Brilliant guides

What you need to know and how to do it

When you're working on your computer and come up against a problem that you're unsure how to solve, or want to accomplish something in an application that you aren't sure how to do, where do you look? Manuals and traditional training guides are usually too big and unwieldy and are intended to be used as end-to-end training resources, making it hard to get to the info you need right away without having to wade through pages of background information that you just don't need at that moment – and helplines are rarely that helpful!

Brilliant guides have been developed to allow you to find the info you need easily and without fuss and guide you through the task using a highly visual, step-by-step approach – providing exactly what you need to know when you need it!

Brilliant guides provide the quick easy-to-access information that you need, using a table of contents and troubleshooting guide to help you find exactly what you need to know, and then presenting each task in a visual manner. Numbered steps guide you through each task or problem, using numerous screenshots to illustrate each step. Added features include 'See also...' boxes that point you to related tasks and information in the book, while 'Did you know?' sections alert you to relevant expert tips, tricks and advice to further expand your skills and knowledge.

In addition to covering all major office PC applications, and related computing subjects, the *Brilliant* series also contains titles that will help you in every aspect of your working life, such as writing the perfect CV, answering the toughest interview questions and moving on in your career.

Brilliant guides are the light at the end of the tunnel when you are faced with any minor or major task.

Publisher's acknowledgements

The author and publisher would like to thank the following for permission to reproduce the material in this book:

National Statistic screenshots reproduced under the terms of the Click-Use Licence; Microsoft product screen shots reprinted with permission from Microsoft Corporation; Pearson screenshots provided by Pearson Plc.

In some instances we have been unable to trace the owners of copyright material, and we would appreciate any information that would enable us to do so.

Author's acknowledgement

The author would like to thank Robert Brent for creating exercises and helping prepare content for this book.

About the author

Greg Holden recently became a member of the Over 50s himself. He has written nearly 40 books on computers and the Internet. His books explore a variety of Microsoft Office products as well as how to operating an online business.

Microsoft®

Brilliant Excel 2007

Tips & Tricks

Gre

PEAR

Pren

Harlow, En
Tokyo • Se

Pearson Education Limited
Edinburgh Gate
Harlow CM20 2JE
United Kingdom
Tel: +44 (0)1279 623623
Fax: +44 (0)1279 431059
Website: www.pearsoned.co.uk

First edition published in Great Britain in 2009

© Greg Holden 2009

The right of Greg Holden to be identified as author
of this work has been asserted by him in accordance
with the Copyright, Designs and Patents Act 1988.

ISBN: 978-0-273-71934-2

British Library Cataloguing-in-Publication Data
A CIP catalogue record for this book is available from the British Library

Library of Congress Cataloging-in-Publication Data
Holden, Greg.
   Brilliant Microsoft Excel 2007 : tips & tricks / Greg Holden
      p. cm.
   Includes bibliographical reference and index.
   ISBN 978-0-273-71934-2 (pbk. : alk. paper) 1. Microsoft Excel (computer file) 2.
Business--Computer programs. 3. Electronic spreadsheets. I. Title.

   HF5548.4.M523H676 2009
   005.54--dc22   2002042268

10 9 8 7 6 5 4 3 2 1
12 11 10 09 08

Set in 11pt Arial Condensed by 30
Printed by Ashford Colour Press Ltd, Gosport, Hants

The Publisher's policy is to use paper manufactured from sustainable forests.

Contents

i

Introduction

Welcome to *Brilliant Excel Tips & Tricks*, a visual quick reference book that shows you how to build on your existing Excel skills to use and develop the more advanced features and functions of Microsoft Excel 2007. It will teach you all of the the insider tips and tricks that will help you use Microsoft Excel 2007 better and more efficiently, but that you don't have time to develop or work out for yourself – learn to do it better and faster from those who know how!

Find what you need to know – when you need it

You don't have to read this book in any particular order. We've designed the book so that you can jump in, get the information you need, and jump out. To find the information that you need, just look up the task in the table of contents or Troubleshooting guide, and turn to the page listed. Read the task introduction, follow the step-by-step instructions along with the illustration and you're done.

How this book works

Each task is presented with step-by-step instructions in one column and screen illustrations in the other. This arrangement lets you focus on a single task without having to turn the pages too often.

Step-by-step instructions

This book provides concise step-by-step instructions that show you how to accomplish a task. Each set of instructions includes illustrations that directly correspond to the easy-to-read steps. Eye-catching text features provide additional helpful information in bite-sized chunks to help you work more efficiently or to teach you more in-depth information. The 'For your information' feature provides tips and techniques to help you work smarter, while the 'See also' cross-references lead you to other parts of the book containing related information about the task. Essential information is highlighted in 'Did you know' boxes that will ensure you don't miss any vital suggestions and advice.

Troubleshooting guide

This book offers quick and easy ways to diagnose and solve common problems that you might encounter, using the Troubleshooting guide. The problems are grouped into categories that are presented alphabetically.

Spelling

We have used UK spelling conventions throughout this book. You may therefore notice some inconsistencies between the text and the software on your computer which is likely to have been developed in the USA. We have however adopted US spelling for the words 'disk' and 'program' as these are commonly accepted throughout the world.

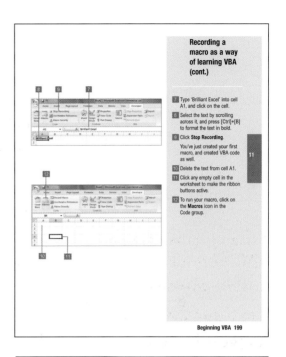

Recording a macro as a way of learning VBA (cont.)

7 Type 'Brilliant Excel' into cell A1, and click on the cell.

8 Select the text by scrolling across it, and press [Ctrl]+[B] to format the text in bold.

9 Click **Stop Recording**.

You've just created your first macro, and created VBA code as well.

10 Delete the text from cell A1.

11 Click any empty cell in the worksheet to make the ribbon buttons active.

12 To run your macro, click on the **Macros** icon in the Code group.

Beginning VBA **199**

Text shortcuts and tips

Introduction

It's true, Excel® isn't primarily intended for formatting text. It's there to enable you to work with numbers, formulas, and data of all sorts. Nevertheless, many times you'll want to devote one column in your workbook to text. Understanding how to format and work with text in general is important. And precisely because you're not using Excel to work primarily with text, shortcuts and tips become especially important. In this chapter, you'll examine some simple steps you can follow to make working with text easier in Excel. That way, you can spend more time analysing the data you're tracking.

What you'll do

Perform a word count in an individual cell

Count specific characters in cells

Change text alignment in cells

Make text wrap in a cell

Change the default font

Change text to uppercase or lowercase

Use Find and Replace

Use Find and Replace on all workbook sheets

Select only cells that contain text

Format only cells that contain text

Extract the first or last word in a cell

Add comments to a cell

Cause comments to appear continuously

Text in Excel 2007

Data is what makes Excel such a valuable tool both in the home and in the workplace, but text labels and other supporting information are what make the data understandable. When you talk about text in Excel, you talk about *strings*. The basic way to edit and format text in Excel is to choose options from the ribbon or type keyboard shortcuts ([Ctrl]+[B] for Bold, [Ctrl]+[F] for Find, for instance). But the best text-related tricks make use of functions. These are commands that are built into Excel and that you can use to perform actions on worksheet contents. You'll find a list of functions on the Formulas tab, as shown below.

Here are a few examples of what the functions can do:

- The CLEAN function removes any nonprintable characters from text.

- The LEFT function finds the character on the left edge of the string; the RIGHT function finds the character on the right edge.

- The UPPER and LOWER functions let you restrict an operation only to upper- or lower-case text.

- LEN lets you record the length of a text string, while SUBSTITUTE lets you record the number of occurrences of a specific text string.

- TRIM removes blank spaces from text; it's useful when counting characters.

- You'll find a list of worksheet functions on the Microsoft website, at **http://office.microsoft.com/en-us/excel/ HP100791861033.aspx.**

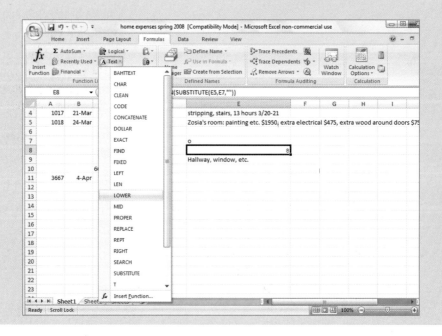

The LEN function is one of several that let you work with text in a workbook. LEN enables you to count the number of characters in a text string. For instance, if a given cell contains a substantial amount of text, it can be difficult to scroll through the text and perform a word count to make sure the contents are within any length limits that have been set. By creating a simple formula, Excel can do the work for you.

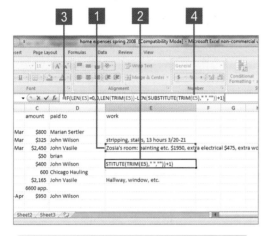

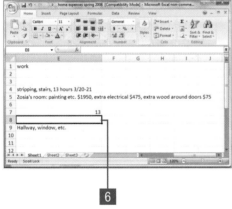

1 Make a note of the location of the cell that contains the text you want to count.

2 Click the cell where you want to locate the function.

3 Type the following:

    =IF(LEN

4 Next, type the cell number of the cell that contains the text you want to count. For instance, if the cell is E5, type:

    =IF(LEN(E5)=0,0,LEN
    (TRIM(E5))-
    LEN(SUBSTITUTE
    (TRIM(E5),"",""))
    +1)

5 Press [Enter] .

6 Make a note of the number of words that appears in the cell you chose for the formula.

?

Did you know?

Functions are commands that are built into Microsoft Excel. They let you perform calculations or other operations on spreadsheet data. IF functions, for instance, let you test whether a condition is true or false. SUM lets you add up values in a selected group of cells. LEN differs from others in that it requires a string rather than a range. A related function, LENB, counts the number of bytes used to represent the characters in a string.

Counting specific characters in cells

Most of the time, you'll probably want to count all of the text in a cell. But in certain specialised situations, you might want to count specific characters. You might want to record all instances of the letter A, or more likely, all instances of the pound symbol (£). First, isolate the character you want to count. Then apply a function that combines LEN and SUBSTITUTE.

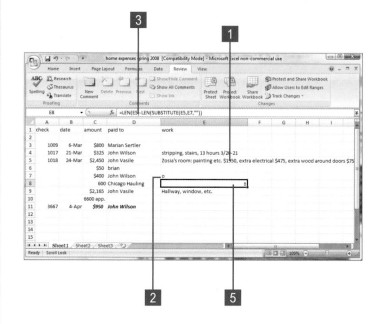

1 Make a note of the location of the cell that contains the text you want to count.

2 Click the cell where you want to locate the function. Type the character you want to count.

3 Type the following:

```
=LEN(A1)-
LEN(SUBSTITUTE(A1,A2
,""))
```

Substitute the number of the cell where you typed the character for A2. Substitute the number of the cell that contains the text you want to count for A1.

4 Press [Enter].

5 Make a note of the number of words that appears in the cell you chose for the formula.

You've probably noticed that, when you start to enter text in Excel, two things happen: the text doesn't wrap, and the text is aligned at the bottom of the cell. In most cases this isn't a problem. But when you attempt to type text of any length in a cell, you're going to want to make some changes. This task shows you how to adjust alignment; the one that follows covers text wrap.

1 Select the cells you want to format.

2 Click the arrow next to Alignment.

3 Click the drop-down arrow next to Vertical.

4 Choose Top.

5 Click **OK.**

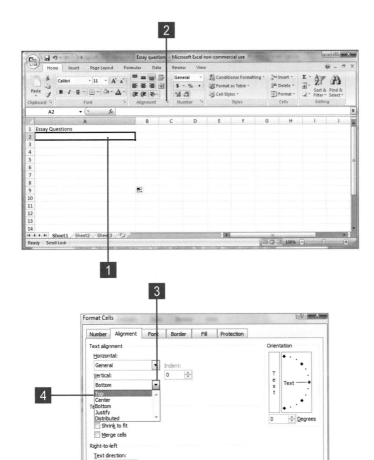

Making text wrap in a cell

When text wraps, it breaks at the right-hand margin of the container in which it is contained, whether that is a column, a text file or a cell. The text then resumes on the next line. By default, text doesn't wrap in Excel. Instead, you have the ability to make text wrap on a cell-by-cell basis. This gives you the flexibility to make text wrap in one cell and not wrap in an adjacent one. First, you need to widen the cell to make the text more readable.

1 Click the cell you want to format.

2 Click **Format**.

3 Type a reasonable number of pixels for the new width of the cell.

4 Click **OK**.

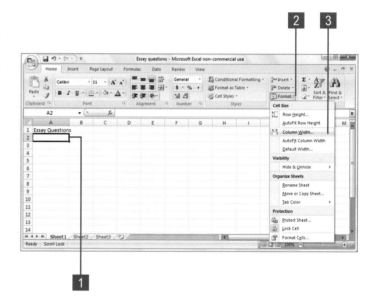

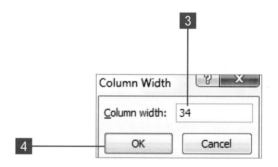

A font is a set of characters that is used to present text. Times, Arial and Helvetica are among common fonts used in a Windows environment. By default, Excel doesn't assign a name to a font. Instead, the text you type is given the generic designation BODY FONT. The actual font chosen is then determined by the theme used by the worksheet. If you use themes, you should leave the BODY FONT designation alone. But if you don't want to use a theme, you can assign your own default font for use in all of your workbooks.

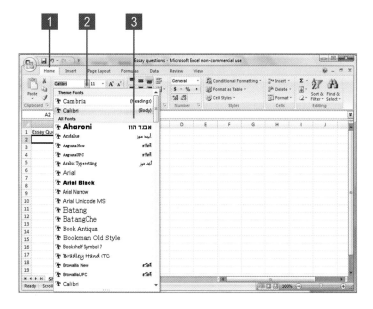

1 Click **Home** if necessary.

2 Click the **drop-down arrow** next to the current font.

3 Inspect the font list and choose the one you want.

For your information

You need to inspect the font list first because it provides you with visual previews of fonts you can choose from. The dialogue box you use to specify the default font does not contain previews, so it's hard to make an informed selection.

Changing the default font (cont.)

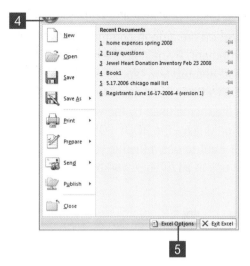

4 Click the **Office** icon.

5 Choose Excel Options.

6 Click **Popular**.

7 Choose a font from this drop-down list.

8 Click **OK**.

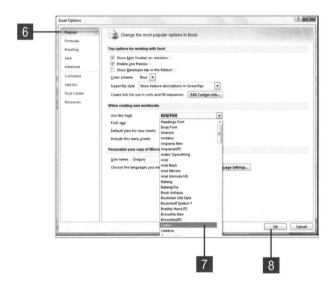

Did you know?

The Popular list of Excel options lets you specify a number of other useful default settings for workbooks you create. You can choose a different font size as well as a font, for instance. You can also choose a different default colour scheme, a default view, and the number of sheets to appear in each new workbook after it is created.

Why go through the time-consuming process of selecting text and changing it from uppercase to lowercase? You can do it by using one of two functions that are built into Excel for just this purpose. Their actions should be clear to you: LOWER makes the text in one cell lowercase, while UPPER makes it uppercase.

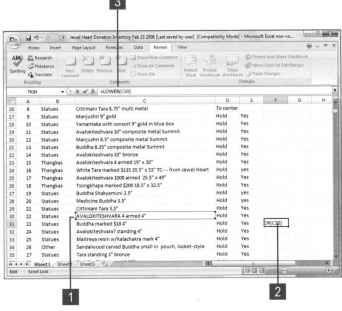

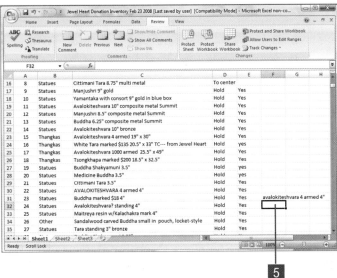

1 Note the location of the cell that contains the uppercase text – for this example, cell C30.

2 Click the cell where you want to locate the function.

3 Type the following function:

```
=LOWER(C30)
```

4 Press [Enter].

5 Copy the lowercase text that appears by highlighting it; press [Ctrl] + [X] to cut it to the clipboard so you can paste it over the uppercase text.

Using Find and Replace

Find and Replace is one of the most useful utilities in any application. Excel enables you to search for and replace labels and values. You can also use Find and Replace to search for text strings and replace them, either individually or all at once.

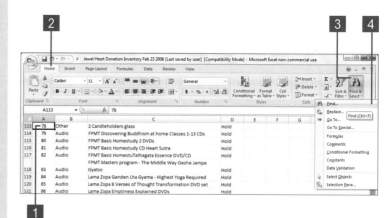

Searching for a string

1. Click at the point where you want to begin searching. If you want to search the whole worksheet, click at the beginning.

2. Click **Home** if necessary.

3. Click **Find & Select**.

4. Choose Find.

5. Type the text string you want to find.

6. Click **Find Next** to find subsequent instances of the string, one at a time.

7. Click **Find All** to produce a list of search results.

8. Click **Close**.

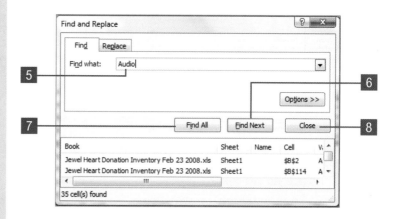

Did you know?

You can use wild cards in the text search. The asterisk (*) can stand for any number of characters and you can enter it either before or after a string. For example, *ing will find *king* and *string*. The question mark (?) stands for a single character: a search for T?N will find TEN or TAN, for instance.

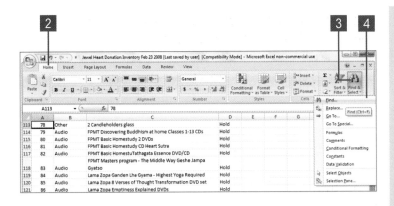

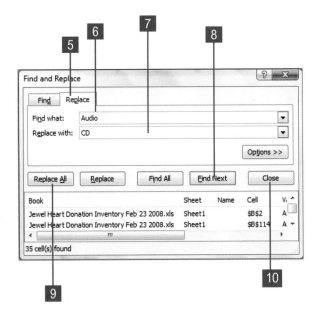

Replacing text strings

1 Click at the point where you want to begin searching. If you want to search the whole worksheet, click at the beginning.

2 Click **Home** if necessary.

3 Click **Find & Select**.

4 Choose Find.

5 Click the **Replace** tab.

6 Type the text string you want to find.

7 Type the text string you want to replace the text you find.

8 Click **Find Next** to start the search, and keep clicking **Find Next** to locate the next instance of the search text.

9 Click **Replace** to replace the text, or **Replace All** to replace all instances throughout the document.

10 Click **Close**.

For your information

Keyboard shortcuts streamline the process of finding and replacing text. Press [Ctrl]+[F] to find text. To replace a string, press [Ctrl]+[H] or click **Replace** from the Edit menu. To find text backwards, press [Ctrl], [Shift]+[F]; to replace text backwards, press [Ctrl], [Shift]+[H].

Using Find and Replace on all workbook sheets

A single shortcut key allows you to extend the power of Find and Replace to all sheets in a workbook at the same time.

1 Right-click the sheet tab and, from the context menu, choose Select All Sheets.

2 Click **Find & Select**.

3 Choose **Find** or **Replace**.

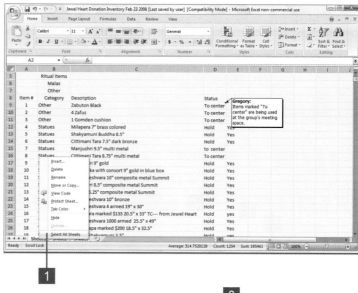

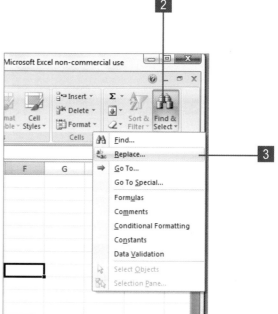

It can be helpful to select only the cells that contain text so you can format them exclusively. Once selected, you can lock the cells or delete them. More importantly, you can format them all at once: you can change the typeface or size, or apply bold and italic formatting. When you have dozens or hundreds of cells that contain only text, it can be a huge timesaver to format them all with a single menu command.

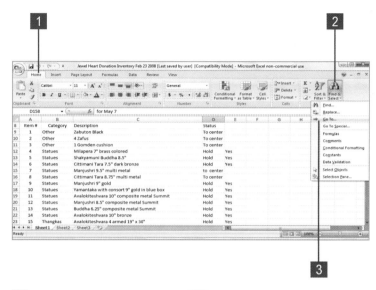

1 Click the **Home** tab if necessary.

2 Click **Find & Select**.

3 Click **Go To**.

4 Click **Special**...

5 Click **Constants**.

6 Click **OK**.

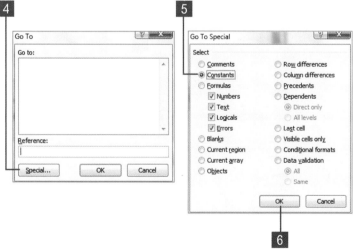

Formatting only cells that contain text

Suppose you select adjacent cells, some of which contain text and some that contain numbers. If you want to change only the text, you can do it by applying the ISTEXT function.

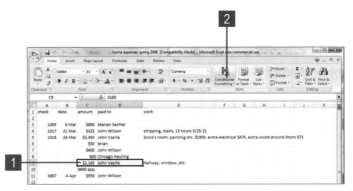

1 Select the adjacent cells.

2 Click **Conditional Formatting**.

3 Choose New Rule.

4 Click **Use a formula to determine which cells to format**.

5 Type:

=ISTEXT(A1)

6 Click **Format... .**

7 Choose one or more formatting attributes.

8 Click **OK**.

9 Click **OK** to close New Formatting Rule.

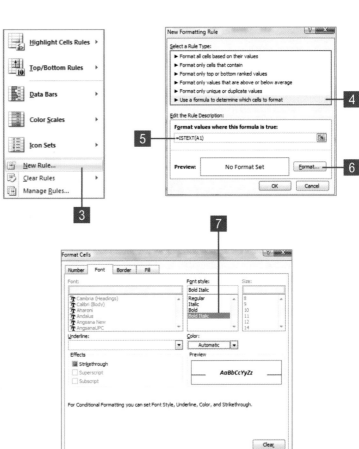

A formula can help you extract the first or last word in a cell that contains text. Different formulas are needed depending on whether you want the first or last word in a cell.

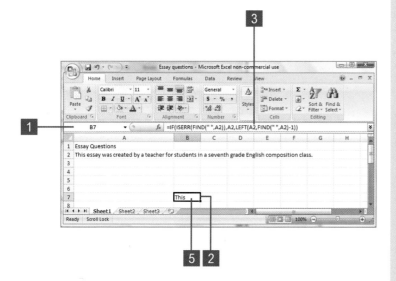

Extract the first word

1 Make a note of the location of the cell that contains the text you want to extract.

2 Click the cell where you want to locate the function.

3 Type the following:

```
=IF(ISERR(FIND("",
A1)),A1,LEFT(A1,FIND
("",A1)-1))
```

Substitute the cell number of the cell that contains the text you want to count for A1.

4 Press [Enter].

5 Make a note of the word that was extracted.

Extracting the first or last word in a cell (cont.)

Extract the last word

1 Make a note of the location of the cell that contains the text you want to extract.

2 Click the cell where you want to locate the function.

3 Type the following:

```
=RIGHT(A1,LEN(A1)-
FIND("*",SUBSTITUTE
(A1,"","*",LEN(A1)-
LEN(SUBSTITUTE(A1,
"","")))))
```

Substitute the cell number of the cell that contains the text you want to count for A1.

4 Press [Enter].

5 Make a note of the word that was extracted.

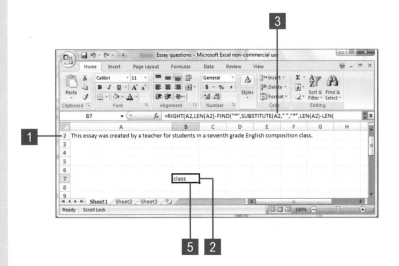

Sometimes, it's useful to add instructions or observations in the form of a comment. Comments help tell viewers what to look for in a cell; they might also instruct someone on how to enter data or otherwise work with a cell. When you add a comment, a red triangle appears in the cell. When you or someone else hovers the mouse pointer over the triangle, the comment appears.

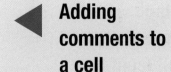

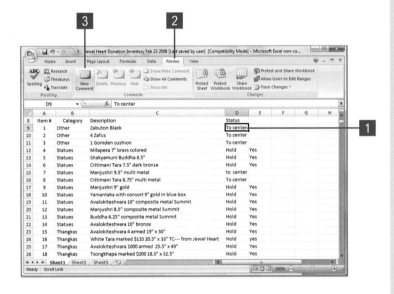

Adding the comment

1 Select the cell that you want to contain a comment.

2 Click the **Review** tab.

3 Click **New Comment**.

4 Backspace to delete your name if you don't want it to appear.

5 Type your comment.

6 Click one of the resize handles to change the size of the comment box.

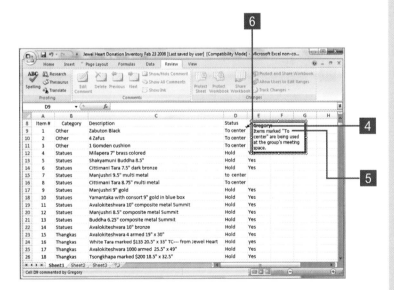

Did you know?

You can also right-click a cell and choose New Comment to add a comment to it.

Adding comments to a cell (cont.)

Formatting the comment

1. Right-click the border around the comment.

2. Choose Format Comment from the context menu.

3. Change the font and alignment if needed.

4. Assign a colour to the comment to make it stand out.

5. Click **OK**.

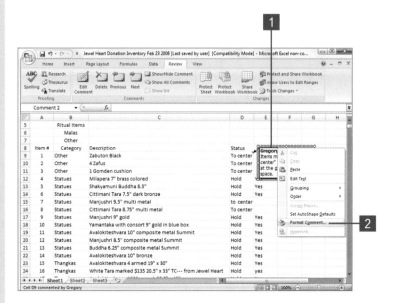

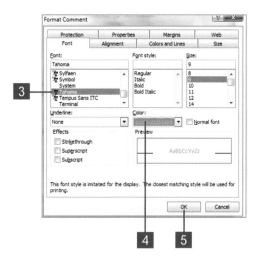

By default, Excel does not display comments. Rather, you need to hover your mouse pointer over the red triangle to view the comment. The tiny red triangle that appears in a cell to let readers know there's a comment present is pretty inconspicuous. For important notes, you can make comments appear on screen permanently. That way, no one will miss them.

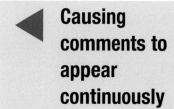
1 Right-click in the cell that contains a comment.

2 Choose Show/Hide Comments.

Tips for working with data and tables

2

Introduction

Data is, of course, the coin of the realm when it comes to Microsoft Excel. Anything you can find to make working with Excel go more quickly will help you focus on interpreting the data. Tables make working with data easier. Turning a range of cells into a table helps you manage and analyse information independently from other data in a worksheet. This chapter helps you work with the data more efficiently so you can perform the calculations you need and move on to other essential tasks.

Some of the tasks in this chapter use a sample spreadsheet called Data_Format.xlsx that you can download from the Pearson website (**http://www.pearson.com/**). There are some obvious problems with this data; before it can be sorted or processed, it needs to be prepared in the proper format.

Formatting in Excel 2007

As anyone familiar with Excel knows, good formatting can mean the difference between a heap of incoherent data and a spreadsheet that tells you what you want to know in a way that's both intuitive and easy to modify. Excel 2007 includes applications that you'll remember from previous versions of Excel, such as the invaluable cell formatting tools, for example, including Number, Alignment, Font, etc., that are accessed by pressing [Ctrl]+[1].

Excel 2007 offers a whole new range of tools, however, that is easily and intuitively accessed from the ribbon.

Among the many tools listed under the Home tab, you will find different formatting options on the Styles pane. It was possible to carry out most of these tasks in previous versions of Excel, but Excel 2007 makes it all much easier, more efficient and intuitive than ever before.

Format as Table

Choose the Format as Table pane, and you will be presented with a broad selection of pre-designed tables ranging in colour and style. You can also apply this to an existing table and give a designated set of cells a new table style, or maybe you want to create your own custom table. Select New Table Style, and you will find a dialogue from which you can choose practically any configuration under the sun to create a custom table that can also be saved and reused later if you wish.

Conditional formatting

This powerful feature allows you to quickly highlight certain data based on a set of criteria that you apply to it. You can choose from a wide array of formatting possibilities, such as scaling it from high to low, highlighting duplicate values, choosing the top ten items, etc., or create your own rules, which can also be used later. You can choose to represent data variations using Icon Sets, Color Scales or Data Bars. This can be particularly handy when you have vast data tables, but you just want to quickly indicate a trend. Using Color Scales, for example, you could represent your cells with a scale from blue to red, where the lower a cell's value, the bluer it is, and the higher its value, the redder it is. A viewer familiar with your parameters would glean an indication of your data distribution from a single glance at your spreadsheet. The Icon Sets can also be updated in real time, giving you a powerful visual indicator of your data's activity. One way to put this to use would be to have an icon assigned to your cells that is red if its respective cell's data is decreasing and green if it is increasing. If you click on the Cell Styles pane, you can change the colours, text styles, headers, etc.

This website offers a helpful video demonstration of conditional formatting:
http://www.microsoft.com/downloads/details.aspx?FamilyId=4BDAEDA8-A6C3-4D4E-9516-B6026850CC43&displaylang=en

Formatting in Excel 2007 (cont.)

A helpful walkthrough of formatting in Excel can be found here:
http://office.microsoft.com/en-us/excel/
HA100137691033.aspx?pid=CH100648351033

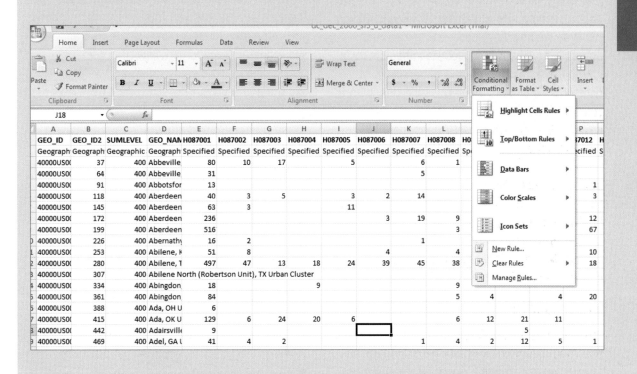

Understanding data mining

Data mining is the science of analysing large sets of data. It is a relatively recent term, but a practice that is essentially no different from the task that has been performed by data analysts for years. What differentiates data mining from previously existing forms of data analysis is the unprecedented size of datasets available today. Because we now have access to gargantuan amounts of data, it has become infeasible for a lone human to sift through it all; analysis of datasets this large is made possible only with the aid of powerful and sophisticated computer-assisted automation. Government agencies, private enterprises and scientific organisations have all quickly become aware of the possibilities that this type of database analysis creates.

The US Army, for example, has claimed that data mining was the primary method used in identifying certain hijackers from the 11 September 2001 terrorist attacks, and it is such a common practice in modern business that there has been a commoditisation of data, leading to the rise of companies and specialists for whom data mining is fast becoming an industry in and of itself. Some worry about the implications regarding basic rights to privacy, and the ongoing debates and legal battles surrounding this issue seem to be only the beginning for this new field which is becoming an increasingly ubiquitous part of everyday life.

This is all fine and good for the heavy hitters out there, of course, but you may be wondering how you as an individual can participate. The answer lies in the unprecedented ease of access to public data that we enjoy today, and we will explore some ways in which Excel 2007 can be used as a data mining tool later in the chapter. It would be frivolous to attempt a comprehensive list of places online where data can be accessed, but here are a few sites to get you started and get you thinking about the kind of data that is made available and the ways it is presented and accessed online.

- Neighbourhood Statistics: **http://www.neighbourhood.statistics.gov.uk/dissemination/Download1.do**.
- Nomis Official Labour Market Statistics: **https://www.nomisweb.co.uk/home/census2001.asp**.
- Alexa the Web Information Company: **http://www.alexa.com/**.

Excel serves as a useful tool when you need to accept data from one application, format it, and move it along to another application such as an Access™ database. But what happens when you *don't* want to automatically format some of that data? Suppose you need to preserve a zero at the beginning of a number such as a post code. Excel doesn't recognise the number in the post code field of the example as a post code. You need to tell Excel not to strip out the leading zero. You do this when you first import the data into Excel using the Text Import Wizard.

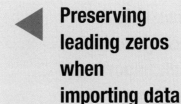

Preserving leading zeros when importing data

1 Click the **Office** button.

2 Click **Open**.

3 Choose All Files.

4 Double-click the text file that contains the data you want.

5 When the Text Import Wizard opens, click **Delimited**.

6 Click **Next**.

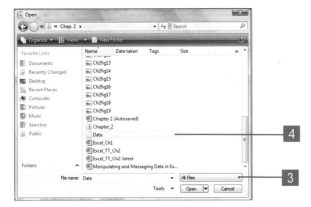

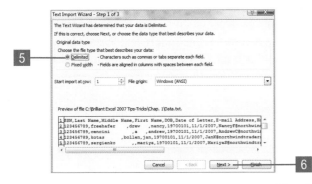

Preserving leading zeros when importing data (cont.)

7 Choose comma as the delimiter.

8 Click **Next**.

9 Select the Post Code field.

10 Select text.

11 Click **Finish**.

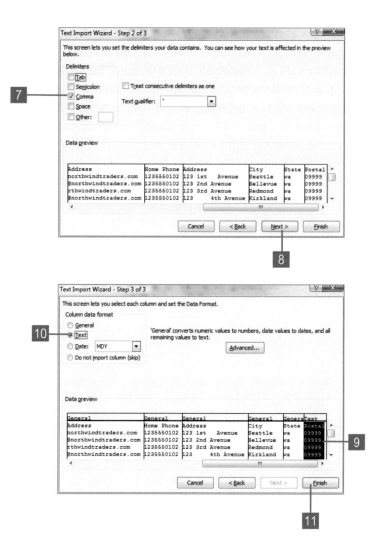

Did You Know?

When importing text, you could also choose a comma or another character, such as tab, as the delimiter. But if you choose a comma, the Import Text Wizard lets you select one field at a time so you can format it individually.

Sometimes, data won't be formatted the way you want it to be right off a website or even when you receive it from a colleague. Notice, for example, that the Social Security Number field in the dataset shown below does not contain the hyphens traditionally used to represent this kind of number.

You can add the formatting yourself in a simple way by following these steps.

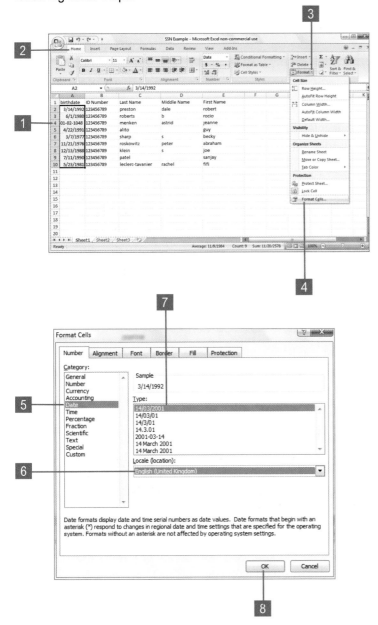

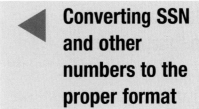
1 Select the cells you want to format.

2 Click **Home** if necessary.

3 Click **Format**.

4 Choose Format Cells, or press [CTRL]+[1] to access the familiar Format Cells dialog box.

5 Under the Number tab, choose Date.

6 Choose English (United Kingdom).

7 Choose the desired type of date.

8 Click **OK**.

Did you know?

You can also choose Custom and create a format for your date or any other type of data, if your preferred data format isn't represented. Note that the data itself is unchanged if you use this method.

Using a formula to format data

If, in contrast to the simple Format Cells method described in the preceding task, you want to actually insert hyphens into values such as American Social Security numbers that your customers across the ocean might have, you will need to use a formula. Essentially, what you are going to do is break up the digits into separate chunks, between which the hyphens will be placed. You can use the MID() function to create a new dataset elsewhere in the spreadsheet that will allow you both to keep the original formatting and have the new formatting as well.

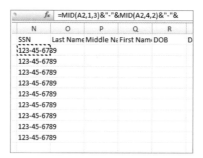

You're going to go all the way to the end of the data to create your new table. So as not to lose your place, copy and paste the header information first by selecting the values from A1 to L1, copying, and pasting starting at N1.

	fx	=MID(A2,1,3)&"-"&MID(A2,4,2)&"-"&			
N	O	P	Q	R	
SSN	Last Name	Middle Na	First Nam	DOB	D
123-45-6789					
123-45-6789					
123-45-6789					
123-45-6789					
123-45-6789					
123-45-6789					
123-45-6789					
123-45-6789					
123-45-6789					

Now that you have your new table, you can write your formula. It helps to think about what, exactly, you're trying to do when writing formulas. This helps you to develop a sense of which formula will be appropriate as you increase your proficiency in Excel. The formula will read as follows:

```
=MID(A2,1,3)&"-"&MID(A2,4,2)&"-"&MID(A2,6,4)
```

Remember that what you've done is to separate the value into three parts that are joined by hyphens. Now all you have to do is paste the formula into N2, copy it, and paste it all the way down your dataset. Notice that, while the cell looks identical to the other cells after simply changing the Number Type, the formula bar now contains your formula.

Proper names can be tricky because there are countless parameters to account for. What if some people have a middle initial but others don't? What if a name is hyphenated? What if capitalisation isn't consistent across your data? Formatting names requires a little more work, but it's by no means an insurmountable task. As we will see, the formula is just a bit more complicated.

In this task, you are going to set the name in the following, traditionally used format (Last Name, First Name, Middle Initial), although once you're familiar with a few basic concepts you can organise them whatever way you want. As in the previous example, the '&' operator will play an important role in this formula because it associates the text (First Name, etc.) with the space and the comma that follow it. The functions used for this task will be LEFT(), which adds the middle initial from the Middle Name category, the TRIM() function, which removes extra spaces, and the PROPER() function, which formats the letter casing to your specifications.

You will once again use the new table you created in the preceding task to the right of the original, but this time, because we're going to combine the columns for First Name, Middle Name and Last Name into one entitled 'Name', these previous three categories can be deleted.

Changing names to the proper format

1 Right-click the unneeded columns and choose Delete.

2

2 In the formula box, enter a formula that incorporates these functions:

```
=PROPER(TRIM(TRIM
(B2)&", "&D2&" "&LEFT
(C2,1)))
```

3 Press [Enter]. The names are now listed last name first, then first name, then middle initial, and, because of the TRIM() function, names with or without a middle initial are listed with appropriate spacing.

f_x	=PROPER(TRIM(TRIM(B9)&", "&D9&" "&LEFT(C9,			

L	M Formula Bar	O	P	Q
:al Code		SSN	Name	DOB	Date of Le I
34		123-45-67;	Preston, Carol D		
34		123-45-67;	Roberts, Jasper B		
34		123-45-67;	Menken, Tom A		
34		123-45-67;	Alito, Macella		
34		123-45-67;	Sharp, Benjamin S		
34		123-45-67;	Roskowitz, Ivan P		
34		123-45-67;	Klein, Elliot S		
34		123-45-67;	Patel, Ashwin		
34		123-45-67;	Leclerc-Tavanier, Jeanne R		

Converting dates to the proper format with a formula

1 Select the cells you want to format.

2 Type the date format shown above in the function box.

3 Press [Enter].

Because dates are numbers, this task should be more straightforward than formatting the names. That said, Excel does not hold the DOB category in our dataset here as dates, but as numeric values. In an earlier task, you learned how to use Format Cells to convert dates for you. In this case, you are going to write a formula that incorporates the MID() function that we've already seen, and this time, we will also use the DATE() function. The formula will look like this:

```
=DATE(MID(E2,1,4),MID(E2,5,2),MID(E2,7,2))
```

The DATE() function formats the value as a date, and the MID() function breaks it up according to your instructions.

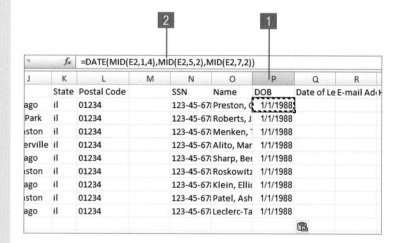

In the interests of getting all your data in the format you want, it makes sense to format email addresses in a uniform way. Email addresses are not case-sensitive, after all, so there's no point in making your data overly complicated for its users. We will use the LOWER() function to render all digits into lowercase.

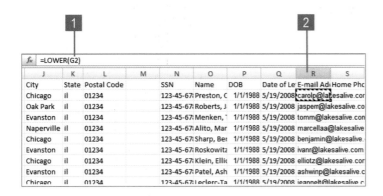

1 Enter the formula =LOWER(G2) into R1 or the cell where your email addresses begin.

2 Copy down the column, giving you uniform email formatting.

Formatting phone numbers with a formula

Once you learn how to add hyphens or other characters to data using a formula, you can apply the same technique to virtually any type of information. In this task, you'll be following the same steps you used to format the SSN, but with a few changes in parameters. As discussed before, it's always a good idea to think about what, exactly, you're trying to do, and how a function will be able to present the values the way you want them. Here, we want phone numbers presented in their traditional format, with the first three digits enclosed by parentheses, and the second three digits separated from the last four digits by a hyphen.

1 Type the appropriate formula in the formula box:

```
="("&MID(H2,1,3)&")
"&MID(H2,4,3)&"-
"&MID(H2,7,4)
```

2 Press [Enter]. The phone numbers are now formatted in an easy-to-read and recognisable way.

1

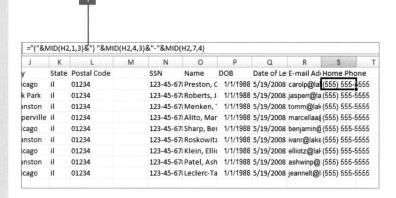

J	K	L	M	N	O	P	Q	R	S	T
	State	Postal Code		SSN	Name	DOB	Date of Le	E-mail Ad	Home Phone	
icago	il	01234		123-45-67	Preston, C	1/1/1988	5/19/2008	carolp@la	(555) 555-5555	
k Park	il	01234		123-45-67	Roberts, J	1/1/1988	5/19/2008	jasperr@la	(555) 555-5555	
nston	il	01234		123-45-67	Menken, 1	1/1/1988	5/19/2008	tomm@lak	(555) 555-5555	
perville	il	01234		123-45-67	Alito, Mar	1/1/1988	5/19/2008	marcellaa(	(555) 555-5555	
icago	il	01234		123-45-67	Sharp, Ber	1/1/1988	5/19/2008	benjamin@	(555) 555-5555	
nston	il	01234		123-45-67	Roskowitz	1/1/1988	5/19/2008	ivanr@lake	(555) 555-5555	
icago	il	01234		123-45-67	Klein, Elli(	1/1/1988	5/19/2008	elliotz@lak	(555) 555-5555	
nston	il	01234		123-45-67	Patel, Ash	1/1/1988	5/19/2008	ashwinp@	(555) 555-5555	
icago	il	01234		123-45-67	Leclerc-Ta	1/1/1988	5/19/2008	jeannelt@l	(555) 555-5555	

Did you know?

If you want to format phone numbers more quickly, you can select the values, hit [CTRL] + [1], go to the Number tab, and choose Special to select Phone Number from a list, or Custom if you want to format it yourself.

As discussed earlier in this chapter, data mining can be a powerful tool in the acquisition and analysis of large datasets. How useful it will be for you depends on what you want to know, and whether you can gain access to the data. It should also be noted that the field of data mining is vast and complex, and providing an exhaustive introduction to it is well beyond the scope of this book. Rather, we will simply go through an example of how data can be obtained online, imported into Excel 2007, and formatted for preliminary analysis.

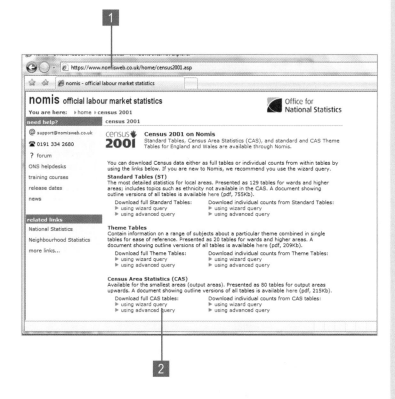

 Data mining with Excel 2007

2

1 Head to a good resource for data acquisition, the nomis official labour market statistics site, at **https://www.nomis web.co.uk/home/census2001. asp**, which was mentioned earlier in the chapter.

2 Under the heading Census Area Statistics (CAS), click **Using Wizard Query** and follow the questionnaire to select the data you want. On the next to last screen, choose the .csv option.

3 On the last screen of the wizard, click the link for the file you want to download.

Data mining with Excel 2007 (cont.)

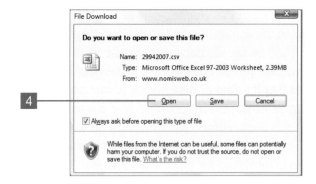

4 When the File Download dialog box appears, click **Open**.

5 Click the **Office** button.

6 Choose Open.

7 Locate the file you downloaded and double-click it to open it.

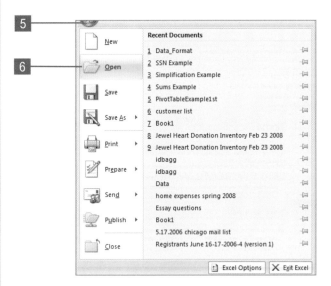

8 It may take a moment to import, but once it's done you have an enormous spreadsheet to play around with. Before we can start applying filters or reorganising the data, select Format as Table, which can be found under the Home tab. This grants us access to some of the data manipulation features, such as Sort, Filter, Text to Columns, etc. Now you can begin to manipulate the data in search of patterns or trends, which is the essence of data mining. While the possibilities are limited only by your imagination, we're going to keep it simple here. Let's find out which age ranges had the highest population in this area. Select the cells in the first table, and then click the **Data** tab.

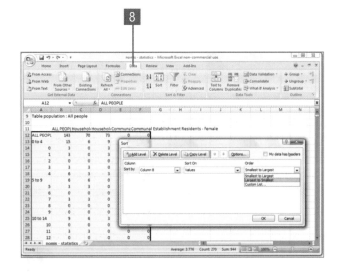

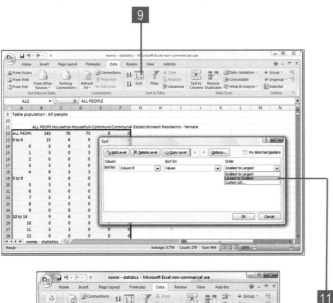

9️⃣ Click **Sort**.

🔟 When a dialog box appears asking if you want to continue with the current selection, click **Sort**.

1️⃣1️⃣ When the Sort dialog box appears, click **Column B**, and click **Largest to Smallest**.

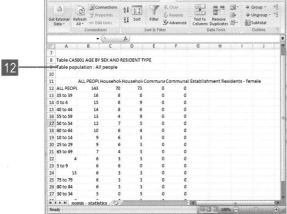

1️⃣2️⃣ Looking over the data now that it's sorted, you can see that in the first area the 35 to 39 age range had 16 people, while the 0 to 4 range was close behind with 15 people, based on the 2001 census. As you can imagine, there is a dizzying array of ways in which data can be analysed once it is imported into a spreadsheet.

For your information

As previously stated, this chapter does not endeavour to present a comprehensive overview of data mining, but rather an introduction to the concept more generally. On that note, Microsoft has recently released SQL Server® Data Mining Add-Ins for Excel 2007. These allow you to link up to the data mining algorithms of Microsoft SQL Server 2005 Analysis Services. More information about obtaining and installing these add-ins can be found at:

http://www.microsoft.com/sql/technologies/dm/addins. mspx.

Watching cells that are not currently on screen

1 Click the **Formulas** tab.

2 Click the **Watch Window** icon. This opens a new dialogue in which you can place the cells you want to watch.

Now that you have a giant spreadsheet brimming with fascinating data, you may come to a realisation: all this data is excellent, but who wants to be scrolling back and forth all over the place to check and double-check various cells? Microsoft has provided a solution in the Watch Window.

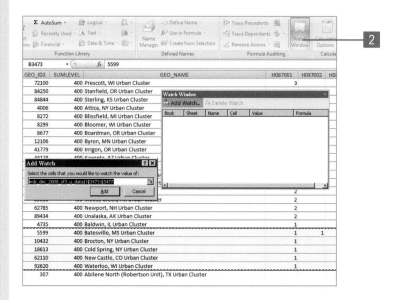

Let's say, for example, that we're working with data in rows 3 through 7 in a table, which represent five geographic regions with the most vacant-for-sale-only homes. You want to be able to compare them to the five geographic regions with the fewest vacant-for-sale-only homes, represented by rows 3473 through 3477. We can only imagine the frustration of constantly scrolling through thousands of rows every time we want to compare. This is where the Watch Window really comes in handy.

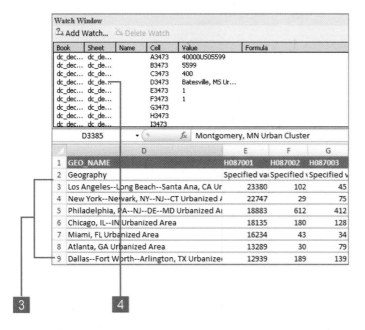

3 Select the lowest-value rows within the data.

4 Position the Watch Window within the main Excel window. Now, monitoring the data side by side is a snap.

Auditing a worksheet

For this final exercise we're going to use the Data_Format spreadsheet you worked on earlier in this chapter. Auditing a worksheet consists of running a check on a spreadsheet to verify that the formulas do not contain errors, and since our first spreadsheet has all the formulas, that is the best choice for learning about this feature.

1. Click the **Office** button.

2. Click **Excel Options**.

3. Choose Advanced.

4. Under the Display options for this workbook section, check every box.

5. Choose All under For objects, show.

6. Click **OK**.

7. Switch back to the worksheet, and select all cells by clicking in the upper left-hand corner.

8. Click the **Formulas** tab.

9. Select Show Formulas. All of the formulas that we've written now appear in their respective cells.

10. Click the **Error Checking** button in the auditing section. The audit assures us that all of our formulas are correct, and we can continue working with the spreadsheet, or present our data with confidence that there are no formula errors.

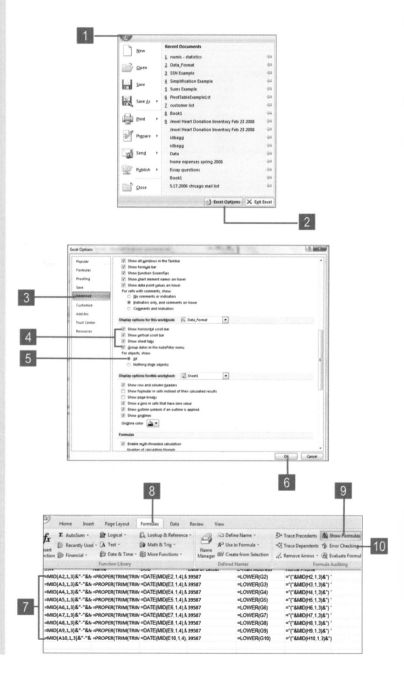

Working with queries

3

Introduction

Many people who use Excel every day have never heard of a query, or if they have, they have never implemented one into their workflow within the Excel environment. Queries, however, can not only help to make what you're doing easier, they open up a whole world of abilities and empower you to do things in Excel that you may never have thought of before. Queries are most prevalent in the world of database management, and an Excel spreadsheet can be thought of as a type of database in the sense that it is a repository for information. Database queries can make finding, extracting and updating your Excel data much more convenient and effective, and allows you to automate certain processes. This chapter will show you how easy it is to implement and run queries, improving your workflow as you let Excel bring the data to you.

There are many ways of working with database queries that do not involve Excel, and even within Excel, an important component of queries is connecting to databases and other sources of information. This chapter will stick to the basics, giving you a foundation on which to build up your knowledge of queries more generally. That means that the data source from which we'll be querying information into Excel will be none other than another Excel spreadsheet that we worked on in Chapter 2. This will familiarise you with how queries work, and teach you how to use them, but there really is a whole world outside Excel to explore when it comes to data retrieval, such as importing data from Microsoft Access, Microsoft SQL Server, or using Microsoft SQL Server Analysis Services, to name a few possibilities.

For your information

For more information about your options for connecting and gaining access to other data sources, getting add-ins, and other query-related issues, you can start visiting the websites listed below:

http://office.microsoft.com/en-us/excel/ HA100996641033.aspx?pid=CH100648471033# quhowThumbAboutQuery_2

http://office.microsoft.com/en-us/excel/ HP102017101033.aspx? pid=CH100648471033

A query is a request for information from an external source. In order to make a query, you need to have a connection to that data source. The first task is to configure the data connection that you're going to use in this chapter so you can get started working with queries in Excel.

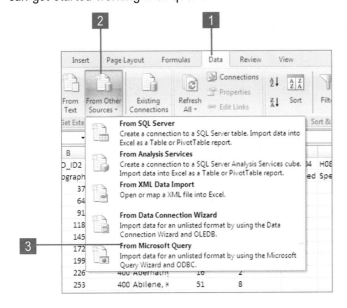

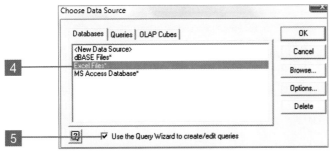

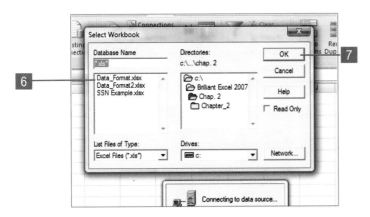

Establishing a data connection

1 Click the **Data** tab.

2 The Get External Data pane provides you with many options for obtaining data. In this case, click **From Other Sources**.

3 Click **From Microsoft Query**.

4 The next dialog box allows you to choose between Databases, Queries and OLAP Cubes. Choose Excel Files.

5 Make sure that Use the Query Wizard to create/edit queries is checked.

6 Now, because you are searching for local data, you'll see that Drives: is set to your C drive, and that you can browse the folders on your hard disk. Also, notice the second, smaller dialogue, indicating that your spreadsheet is connecting to an external data source, which, in this case, is going to be another spreadsheet stored on your hard disk. Select the Excel file called Data_Format, which is the one you created in Chapter 2.

7 Click **OK**.

3

Establishing a data connection (cont.)

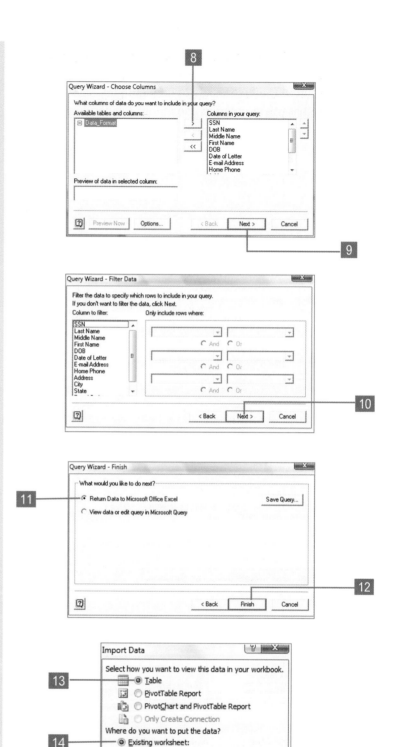

8 The next dialogue will ask you to choose columns, which you can view by clicking the **+ sign** next to the file name. For now, just transfer the entire file over by clicking the **> arrow**.

9 Click **Next**.

10 Click **Next** here and in the next dialog box.

11 Click **Return Data to Microsoft Office Excel** so you can manipulate it as a spreadsheet.

12 Click **Finish**.

13 Click **Table**.

14 Click **Existing Worksheet**.

15 Click **OK**.

Did you know?

OLAP stands for Online Analytical Processing, and is widely used in tasks relating to business administration, such as marketing and sales analysis. You can find more information about these other applications at the olap.com website, **http://www.olap.com**.

Sometimes, you'll try to establish a data connection to a file and Microsoft Query will report that the connection cannot be established. If that is the case, try these quick troubleshooting steps.

1 Open the file to which you are trying to connect.

2 If you see a Security Warning stating that Data connections have been disabled, click **Options**.

3 Click **Enable this content**.

4 Click **OK**.

3

Understanding queries

Quite simply, a query is the type of language that a computer uses to retrieve information from databases. In that sense, the word *query* has essentially the same meaning in the realm of computers as it does in its more traditional sense – strictly speaking, the computer is not doing anything that human beings couldn't theoretically do – a person could query a database by hand given enough time, motivation, and access to data. There's only one problem: you'd have to slog through enormous databases and spreadsheets for days, months or even years trying to find what you need. In fact, the applications that queries have made possible would be well beyond our reach were we to try to replicate the process without computer-assisted automation.

So what are these applications, anyway, and how do computers search databases? One of the most familiar is a web search. When you enter a search into the Google or Yahoo! search engine, you are performing a data query. Your computer is sifting through vast amounts of data to try to find the best match for the information you've requested. This is what's classified, at the most basic level, as an *information retrieval* query language, in contrast to a *database query* language. Whereas queries rely on specific syntax to identify data (i.e. your search will pull up matches for the exact phrase you inputted), an information retrieval query interprets the data in an attempt to best match its findings to your search by weighting and ranking the data it encounters.

The most widely used database query language is SQL. Developed in the 1970s at IBM, it has become the industry standard, and is, consequently, the language that we will be working with here. Don't be intimidated by all this talk of computer languages. We're not doing any hardcore programming, and before you know it, running queries will become one more simple and useful tool among many.

Did you know?

Queries are generally thought of as belonging to one of two categories, **database query** languages and **information retrieval** query languages. Database query languages, the most prevalent of which is SQL, are used in Microsoft Excel and Microsoft Access, for example, to find and track data. Information query languages rely on interpretation rather than actual phrasing, and are more commonly seen in web search engines.

Running a background query is very helpful because it allows us essentially to kill two birds with one stone. While we're plugging away at our spreadsheet, our query can be updating information from whatever data source we've chosen. In the case of the Excel file that we're using here, that could mean, for example, that if, say, someone's address or last name changed in the original spreadsheet, it would be reflected in the data linked to our new spreadsheet. In this task you're going to select cell A2 on which to run a background query, although, as you can imagine, a background query can be run on as many or as few cells as you choose.

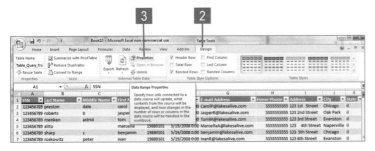

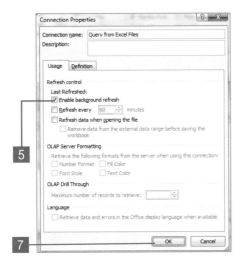

1 To run a query in the background, open the file that has the connection you made earlier in 'Establishing a data connection'.

2 Click the **Design** tab.

3 Under the External Data Table pane, click **Properties**.

4 The External Data Properties dialogue will appear. Click on the icon to the right of the Name field.

5 Make sure the box next to Enable background refresh is checked.

6 Additionally, you can specify how often the background query refreshes, or whether you want it to refresh whenever the program is opened.

7 When you're done, click **OK** here to close this and **OK** to close the previous dialog box.

Did you know?

If you want to do a refresh manually, just uncheck the box next to Enable background refresh, and simply click the **Refresh** icon in the External Table Data pane under the Design tab whenever you want to run your query.

Customising a parameter query

Convenience is a good thing. I sometimes find myself wanting to get a very particular type of information on the fly as I'm working in a spreadsheet. A parameter query lets you do just that by allowing you to enter the information into an easily accessible preset interface. Parameter queries give you the benefit of setting up the way your query will run ahead of time. Then, when you want information, your query will remind you of which kind of data you're looking for. Before you can customise your parameter query, you have to create it, of course. Because you're working in Excel, you will once again use Microsoft Query to link data from another spreadsheet.

1 Follow steps 1 through 10 in 'Establishing a data connection'.

2 This time, when you reach the Query Wizard – Finish dialogue, choose View data or edit query in Microsoft Query instead of returning the data to Excel.

Your data is displayed in Microsoft Query, where you can set up your parameter query. Make sure the Show Criteria icon is selected. It is the sixth icon from the left on the toolbar.

Make sure the Automatically Return Query (or Auto Query, as its tool tip says) icon is not selected.

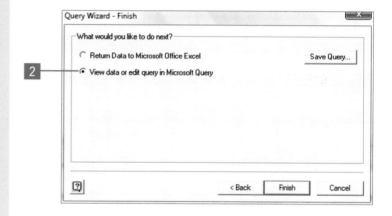

Show criteria

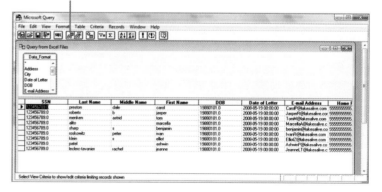

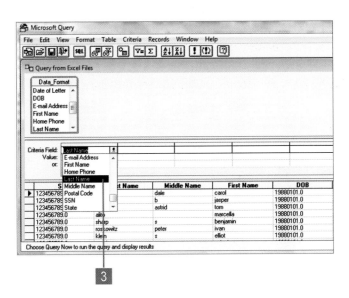

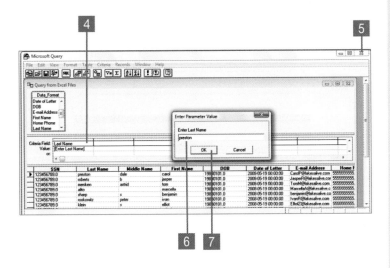

3 Now all that's left is to decide which parameters you want to use. Since this is just a sample spreadsheet we've created, choose Last Name as your parameter. Mouse over the Criteria Field, and choose Last Name from the drop-down list.

4 Type [Enter Last Name] as your custom prompt-to-be in the Value field, making sure to precede and follow the phrase with a bracket.

5 Exit the query by clicking the **Close** box in the upper right-hand corner of the Microsoft Query window.

6 The custom prompt will request a value. Enter 'preston'.

7 Click **OK** to import data for only the first item into your spreadsheet.

Changing the custom prompt for a query

Suppose you're working in your spreadsheet, and instead of having the query ask you to 'enter last name' as it does currently, you want it to say 'choose last name'. It's easy to change such information if it is contained in the spreadsheet you are currently working on. But if the information is contained in another spreadsheet or other remote data source, you have to follow a few simple steps.

1 Select any cell in the spreadsheet that has the connection to the external data source.

2 Click **Data**.

3 Click **Properties**.

4 Click the **Definition** tab.

5 Here, you'll see the location of the Connection string, you'll see the Command text, and you can also browse for new connection files from this dialogue. Click on **Parameters**.

6 You can now see a few options at our disposal. Right now, we're interested in the first field, listed as Prompt for value using the following string. I'm going to enter the text 'choose last name'.

7 Click **OK**. Now, when you refresh the query, this is the instruction you will be given.

8 As you can see, although the query carries out the same task, it requests the information using our new custom prompt.

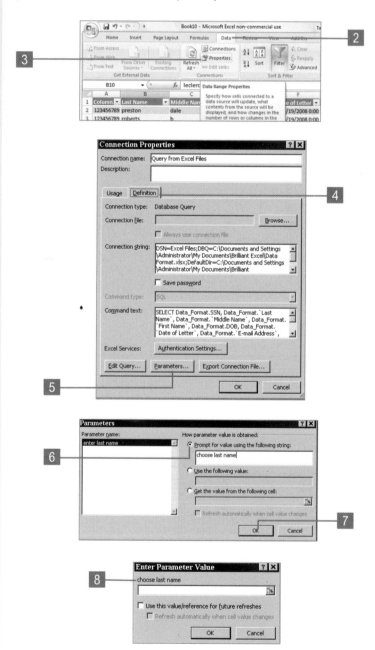

Excel often gives you more than one way to perform a function. The process of adjusting query parameters can also be performed by obtaining data from another cell. You do this in the same Parameters dialog box you used earlier. Follow steps 1 through 3 in the preceding task to open Connection Properties. Then follow these steps.

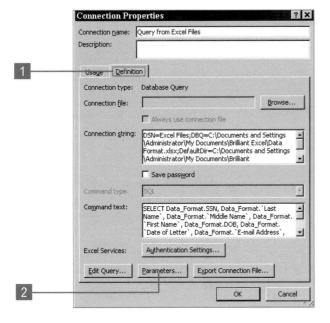

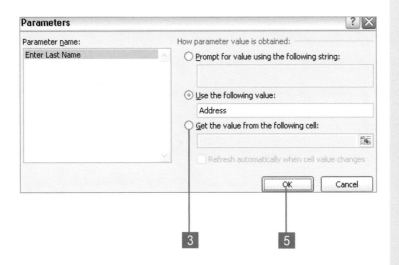

Using cell data as query parameters

1. Click the **Definition** tab.

2. Click **Parameters**.

3. This time, click the button next to Get the value from the following cell.

4. You can type in the coordinates of that cell if you choose, or, by clicking the icon next to the blank field, you can just click on the cell in your spreadsheet that you want to use as your query parameter.

5. Click **OK**. Now, when you hit Refresh All in the Connections pane, only the cell data that you have selected will be updated.

3

Using a constant parameter value for a query

1. Open the Parameters dialog box as described in the preceding task.

2. Click the button next to Use the following value.

3. Type Address (or another value, if you wish) in the field beneath this button. By doing so, you choose 'SSN' as the value that you want to query.

4. Click **OK**.

5. When you return to the database window, if you click **Refresh All** (or when the query refreshes itself automatically in the event that you've set it up to run in the background, as discussed earlier in the chapter), this is the value that will be queried.

Excel gives you a variety of options for tweaking your query to your exact specifications. It may seem a bit tedious now, but just imagine that one day you may be working with a query in Excel, and at one point in your analysis you need to refresh, say, the price of oil, but later, you want to check sales figures at a certain retail location. This is the exact type of thing that is made easier using parameter queries. Once again, we're going to the Parameters dialogue, and this time, we'll customise our query in the Use the following value field.

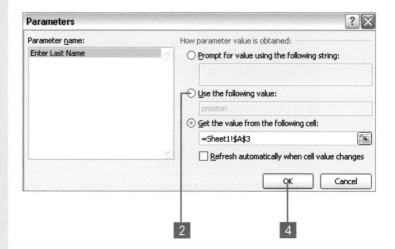

At the beginning of this chapter, you used Microsoft Query to link data from one Excel spreadsheet to another. But you skipped over some of the options that are available for making such connections. There are a variety of ways to build a query to your specifications using the Query Wizard, from which columns and tables you want to use, right down to what values you'll allow for certain data.

Building your own query

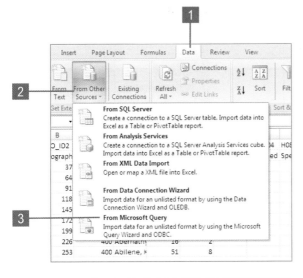

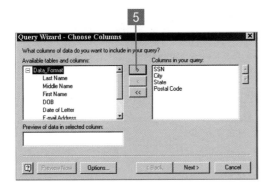

1 Click the **Data** tab.

2 Click **From Other Sources**.

3 Click **From Microsoft Query**.

4 Make sure the Use the Query Wizard to create/edit queries box is checked.

5 Select only the SSN, City, State, and Postal Code fields and click the **right arrow (>)** to move each to the right side of the query screen. If you want to remove them, just select them in the right-hand field, and click the **left arrow (<)** to put them back.

3

Building your own query (cont.)

6 Next, decide which rows to include by selecting the column to filter, and choosing whether to represent only values based on whether they are greater than, less than, equal to, etc. a certain numeric value. And remember that since you're going to be updating information when you refresh your query, this can be very helpful for, say, tracking a stock price: you only want to see a particular stock if the price exceeds a certain amount.

7 The next dialogue lets you sort your data, and decide whether you want it to ascend or descend. In the final dialogue, which should look somewhat familiar by this point, we can save our query, and choose whether to view the data in Microsoft Query or in Microsoft Excel.

8 Choose Return the data to Excel, and as you can see above, only the information that you requested in your custom-built query is displayed.

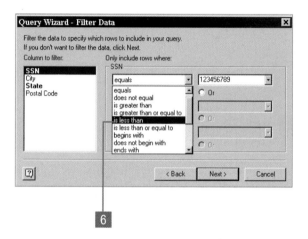

6

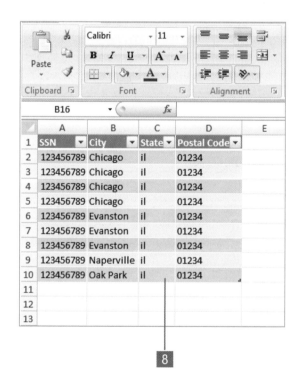

8

52

In this final section on queries, revisit Microsoft Query and look at the other ways it can be used to retrieve data. First of all, Microsoft Query can access many types of databases, including:

- Microsoft SQL Server Analysis Services (OLAP provider)
- Microsoft Office Access
- dBASE
- Microsoft FoxPro
- Microsoft Office Excel
- Oracle
- Paradox
- Text file databases.

This chapter has dealt with queries to Microsoft Excel, but that's really only the tip of the iceberg. The process and concepts behind creating queries are the same no matter which type of database you're accessing. But connecting to data sources can not only be tricky, but it often requires access to be granted or potentially proprietary processes that differ depending on which third-party provider's database you're using. This process often also involves obtaining password and login authentication and can be extremely pricey. For more information, check out Microsoft's website on external data retrieval at:

**http://office.microsoft.com/en-us/excel/HA100996641033.
aspx?pid=CH100648471033**

But remember, data retrieval doesn't have to be just for the pros. As we discussed earlier in the chapter, there are plenty of free online data repositories and feeds.

**Using Microsoft
Query to
retrieve data**

3

Data forms

Introduction

Data forms are easy to implement, and can make your spreadsheets much more powerful. Before you start working with data forms, you're going to learn a little bit about what they are, what they can be used for, how some differ from others, and how different types can be used.

Information is commonly stored in databases, but that doesn't mean your intended users are automatically going to be familiar with your particular database. Let's say you go to your bank's website, and decide you want to start managing your account online. The site won't present you with an enormous database that you have to navigate and make sense of. Rather, the site provides easy-to-use fields that you can fill in, some with drop-down menus, some with a preset selection of items from which to choose, some with scroll bars, etc. With data forms, you can create the same intuitive tools that can be used to interact with your spreadsheet.

What you'll do

Configure Excel 2007 to use data forms

Work with the Quick Access Form icon

Access form controls

Add a list box

Add a list box using form controls

Create a list box using ActiveX controls

Add a combo box

Insert a spinner

Add a scroll bar

Use OFFSET and scroll link in scroll bars

Create a blank user form

Create a custom dialogue box

Excel 2007 and data forms

Excel 2007 gives you several different ways of implementing form controls. The application includes a new Form button that you can embed directly into the ribbon, and which allows you to create very basic data forms in just a few clicks. You can also implement certain form controls that limit the type of data allowed for particular cells, using the Data Validation tool. The most sophisticated and robust application of form controls involves using the Visual Basic® editor. This is how you create your own custom dialogue box with a rich offering of custom design possibilities to choose from.

The two most common types of data form controls, however, are form controls and ActiveX® controls. In Microsoft Excel 2007, these tools are found in the ribbon under the Developer tab.

Form controls and ActiveX controls are very similar in that they perform what appear to be almost identical functions, but just in different ways. In fact, form controls are older, but ActiveX controls resemble the controls used to create UserForms in Visual Basic. The major difference you'll notice is that form controls seem more straightforward, and are created through a relatively robust Format Control dialogue box that is similar to the dialogue system employed by other Excel 2007 applications.

ActiveX controls, on the other hand, have very little in the way of a Format Control dialogue box. Instead, their formatting environment is extensive, and ultimately offers a richer, more robust array of tools for customising your form controls. Moreover, as you will see, once you get comfortable with ActiveX controls, you will find them more convenient for certain tasks. Throughout this chapter you will learn how to use either method in accomplishing a given task.

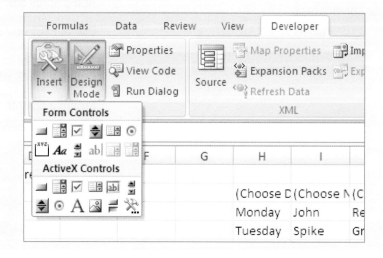

Before you can start working with data forms, you'll need to prepare the spreadsheet. While Excel includes many items in the ribbon when you first open a new spreadsheet, the Data Forms icon isn't one of them – perhaps the average user isn't expected to need something so relatively specialised. In any event, adding the Data Forms icon is easily done.

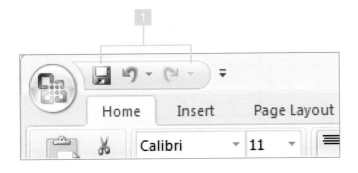

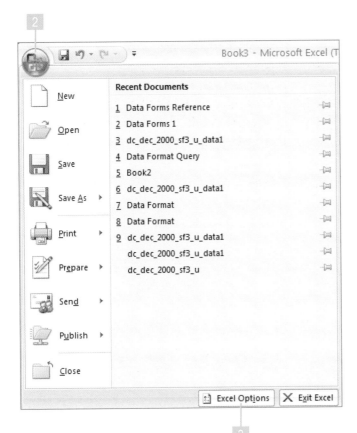

Configuring Excel 2007 to use data forms

1 Note the Quick Access Toolbar. This is where you will be adding the Data Forms icon.

2 Click the **Office** button in the upper left-hand corner.

3 Click **Excel Options** next to the Exit Excel button in the lower-right hand corner.

Data forms 57

Configuring Excel 2007 to use data forms (cont.)

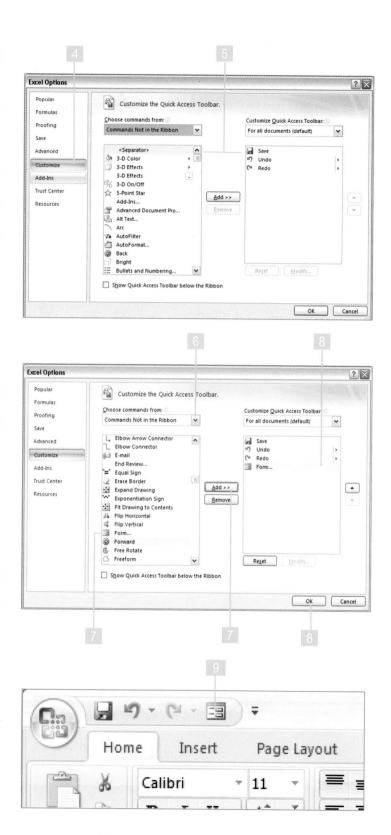

4 Select Customize.

5 You will see two fields with separate scrolling menus beneath them, and the buttons Add and Remove in between them. The field on the left shows what functions you can add to the Quick Access Toolbar. The field on the right shows what is already there, which currently consists of the Save, Undo and Redo buttons.

6 Now, go to the drop-down menu for the Choose commands from field and choose Commands Not in the Ribbon.

7 Scroll down until you see the Form icon, click on it to select it, and click the **Add** button.

8 You should see Form now appear in the Quick Access Toolbar panel on the right, and click **OK**.

9 You should see the Form icon in your Quick Access Toolbar. Remember that any functions you use regularly might be good candidates for adding to the Quick Access Toolbar.

The Quick Access Toolbar Form icon is a new feature, not available in previous versions of Excel. This is the simplest and quickest way to begin working with data forms, and should provide a more tangible illustration of what they are and how they work. It should also help you to start thinking about how they can work for you.

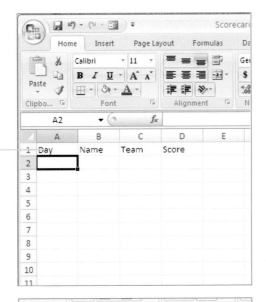

Working with the Quick Access Toolbar Form icon

1 We'll start by creating a very simple spreadsheet. I've opened a new spreadsheet, and saved it under the name, Scorecard. Now, just fill in the information in cells A1 through D1 as indicated in the image below.

2 Before you actually create the data form, fill in some data in row two. This data can be changed, and it doesn't really matter what it is. In fact, we're only doing this to tell Excel that the first row is meant to be a column header so it can intuit how the form should look.

3 Here's where the Form button that we added to the Quick Access Toolbar comes into play. Just select cells A1 through D1 and click on the **Form** button, and a very basic example of a data form will appear. The number of blank fields will correspond to the number of columns, and the column headers will be displayed as labels for the blank fields. Now, just fill in the fields and click **New**, which will take you to the next row. The advantage of this interface is that you don't have to keep scrolling down to fill in the new information.

Accessing forms controls

Form controls are another essential element of the way Excel works with data forms. With them, you can transform an ordinary spreadsheet, amounting to little more than columns and rows of data, into an extraordinary interactive data entry tool. Like the Forms button, these controls may not be displayed when you first open a spreadsheet in Excel 2007. They are found on the Developer tab in the ribbon, so if you don't see the Developer tab, you'll just have to add it, which is done in a similar manner to adding the Form control.

1 Click the **File** button in the upper left-hand corner, and, once again, click on **Excel Options** in the lower right-hand corner.

2 Now click on the first button in the list, **Popular**, and look under the list, Top options for working with Excel.

3 Check the box for Show Developer tab in the Ribbon.

4 Click **OK**, and you should see the Developer tab when you return to the spreadsheet.

5 Click on the **Developer** tab, and you'll see tools such as Visual Basic, Macros, Insert, and Design Mode. We'll talk a little bit about Visual Basic at the end of this chapter and more extensively later in the book. For now, click the **Insert** tab, and you'll see the Form Controls on top and ActiveX Controls on the bottom.

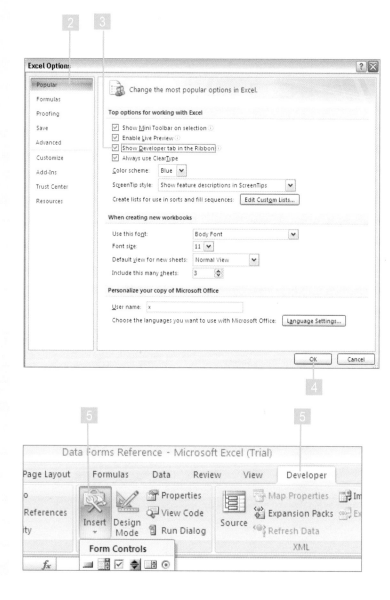

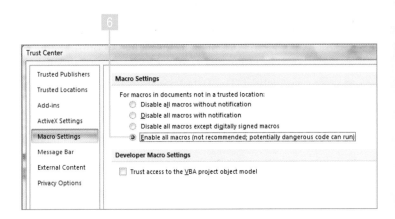

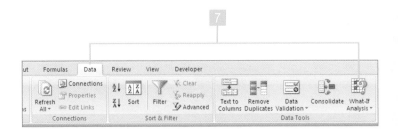

6 Finally, look at the Code group on the left-hand side of the ribbon. Here, you'll see a button labelled Macro Security. This is where you enable or disable macros. If macros are disabled, your form controls won't work. Why would macros be disabled? The answer is that enabling macros can present a security risk to your computer because, since macros are snippets of automated code, they provide a highly accessible way to create and launch viruses. This should not be a concern so long as your spreadsheet is from a trusted source (such as yourself, for instance). If you're trying to execute a command with one of your form controls, and nothing happens, click on the **Macro Security** button, and verify that Enable all macros is selected.

7 There's one more place on the ribbon you'll be going to in this chapter. This time it's on the **Data** tab, and you should see this displayed in the ribbon right from the start. We're interested in the Data Tools group. We'll be using the Data Validation Tools in the next exercise, and, as you'll see, you can use these to create a certain type of data form.

Adding a list box

A list box is a very useful type of form control, and has many possible applications. It allows you to link a data range to a single cell, essentially creating a drop-down menu that lets you select from your dataset within the cell where the data goes. One application of this feature is that it can eliminate the need to scroll long distances over very large spreadsheets and streamline your interface, making data entry simple and convenient.

In addition to the form controls and the ActiveX controls, the aforementioned Data Validation tool can be used to add a list box to your spreadsheet. The Data Validation tool allows you to restrict the type of data that is authorised for a particular cell. If a user enters data that is not allowed by your validation criteria, an error message will appear.

1 First, you'll need to enter some data that you can use to populate your list box. Enter the data into your spreadsheet as seen in the figure.

2 Click on the **Data** tab, and then click on **Data Validation** in the Data Tools group. There are three tabs in the Data Validation dialogue. The first tab, Settings, is the one that we're interested in here. Take a quick look at the other tabs just to see the options presented. The Input Message tab lets you customise the message that appears when a user clicks in a designated cell, while the Error Alert tab lets you customise the dialogue that appears if data not allowed by the validation criteria is entered.

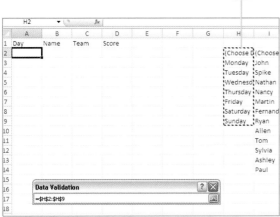

Next, you'll need to configure the Data Validation settings. Click the drop-down menu under the Allow: label, and select List.

Click on the icon in the Source field below it. You will be presented with a collapsed blank field. Now, just select the range that you want your list box to contain, and press [Enter].

Press [Enter] again to view your new list box. You should see an arrow at the edge of your cell, and when you click in the cell, the selected range appears from which you can choose the value you want.

You can AutoFill the list box as far down the column as you want.

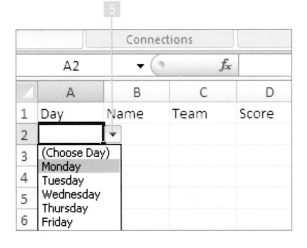

Adding a list box using form controls

Now we're going to look at how to add a list box using the form controls or the ActiveX controls, so you can just select the object you created and delete it. Remember from the introduction that, broadly speaking, form controls are operated through the form control dialogue, whereas ActiveX controls rely on the formatting environment. Don't worry if you are unfamiliar with these terms, you'll soon see what all of this jargon refers to.

1 You're going to start with form controls because they are a little more approachable for the uninitiated, and you'll be using the spreadsheet, Scorecard. Click on the **Insert** button on the Developer tab, and find the button labelled List Box (Form Control) when you hover the icon over it. Your icon will be replaced by a cross-shaped icon. Use this to draw your object in the spreadsheet. It should look like the opposite image.

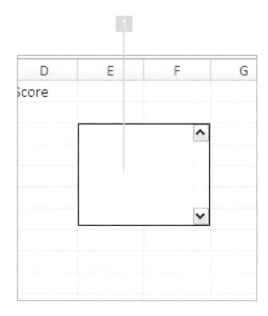

Adding a list box using form controls (cont.)

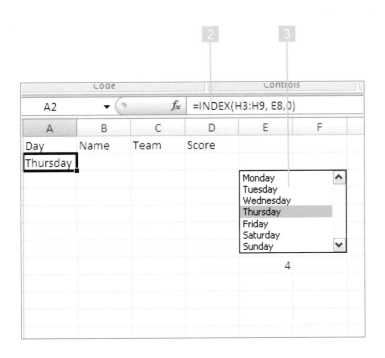

2 Before you proceed to customise your list box, enter the following code in cell A2:

`=INDEX(H3:H9,E8,0)`

This formula will make it so the cell linked to your list box displays the data in the data range. Otherwise, the linked cell would display a number indicating the selected value's position in the list.

3 Now, right-click on the list box object that you've created, and select the Format Control dialogue. You have to choose two elements: the input range, i.e., which data the list box will reference, and the cell link, which is where the data will be displayed. Choose input range H3:H9, and cell link E9. You should now be able to click on your list box, and have your selection appear in A2 (the selected value's position in the list will be displayed in your linked cell, E9).

4

Creating a list box using ActiveX controls

Now you'll make a list box, but this time using the ActiveX controls, so once again, delete the object you just created. This method turns out to be a little more efficient because you don't have to enter a formula in the cell where you want the data displayed. The ActiveX control is preset to do this automatically.

1 Once again, go to the Controls on the Developer tab, and click **Insert**, but this time you'll choose the ListBox in the ActiveX Controls, and again, you'll draw your object as indicated in the image opposite.

As you can see, it looks slightly different from the form controls version, but has the same basic design.

2 Now, right-click on your newly created object, and this time, click **Properties**. The formatting environment dialogue will appear as a list of form control attributes. You can tinker with these if you wish, changing the colour, size, font, etc., but for the purposes of this exercise, we're only worried about the cells linked to your control. Enter A2 in the LinkedCell field, and H3:H9 in the ListFillRange field. You are taking the data in cells H3:H9 and displaying your selection from the list in cell A2. You should see your data range appear in the ListBox, and the selection you click within the object should appear in cell A2.

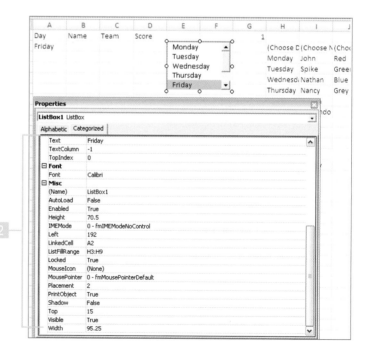

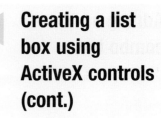

Creating a list box using ActiveX controls (cont.)

3 If you find that you're not able to click inside the object to choose an item from the list, make sure you aren't in Design Mode by clicking the Design Mode button. If that doesn't work, double-check to make sure macros are enabled.

4

Adding a combo box

If you leave the list box you created in the preceding task where it is, you can then move on to add more controls to the spreadsheet. Now that you've seen how the process works, and the difference between form controls and ActiveX controls, the next few tasks should become increasingly familiar. First, you will add a combo box using the form control.

1 Click on the **Insert** button on the Developer tab. Choose Combo Box, and then draw your object beneath the ListBox as shown.

2 We're going to use this control to input data into the Name column. Remember, with form controls, you use the Format Control dialogue to customise your object. As with the list box you created, you will click on the **Control** tab, select the cells from which your data is taken, and the cell link where your data is displayed. Enter the number 12 in the Drop down lines field, because we have twelve names in our spreadsheet.

3 As before, you'll have to use the INDEX function to display your data in the desired field, so enter the following formula in cell B2:

`=INDEX(I3:I14,E12,0)`

Now, cell E12 should display the position of your selection in the list, and cell B2 should display the actual list item.

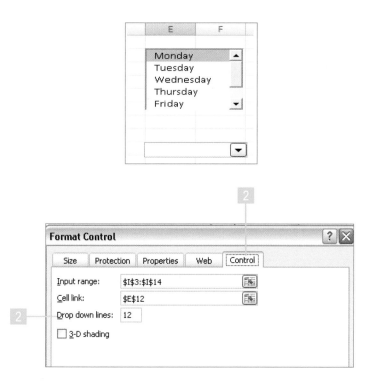

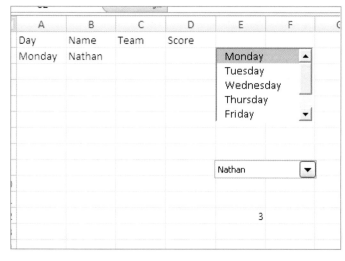

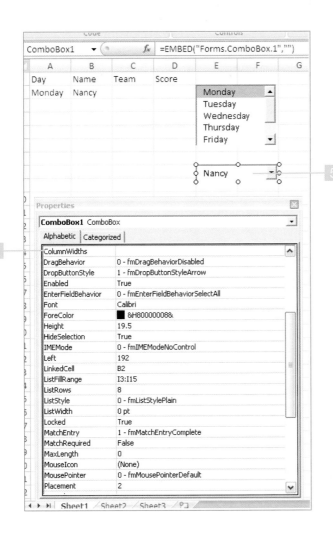

4
Once again, delete the object you just created; and you're going to re-create it using ActiveX controls. You might be sensing a trend here. While it's true that ActiveX controls are ultimately more powerful and flexible, and my personal preference, some report them to be somewhat buggier, which is consistent with their relative newness.

5 Click **Insert** again, and select Combo Box from the ActiveX controls. Draw your object right where you drew the last one. Again, note the similarity between the ActiveX control's appearance and that of the form control.

6 Right-click on the object to access the Properties dialogue. As you've seen, with ActiveX controls, you need to be in Design Mode to edit your object, and you need to exit Design Mode to use it.

Inserting a spinner

Next, you'll insert a spinner, first with the form controls, and then using the ActiveX controls. So go once again to the Controls under the Developer tab and select Format Controls.

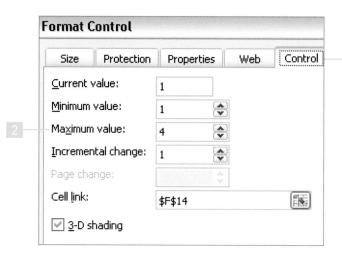

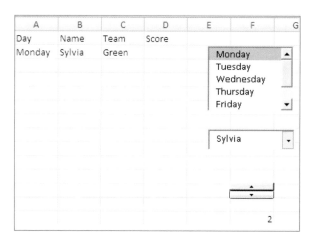

1. In the Control tab, you'll see that the available fields are a little different from what you've seen in the other types of form controls. This is because a spinner performs the more basic task of simply scrolling to and from a linked cell, so all you need to define is essentially how far you want it to scroll and how much of an incremental change you want.

2. Fill in the blanks as indicated. You are entering a maximum value of 4 because we are using the spinner to fill in the Team column, and there are only four teams to choose from. Cell F14 indicates how far from your cell of origin you've moved, and in order to display the desired value in the Team column, insert an INDEX formula in cell C2:

        =INDEX(J3:J6,F14,0)

You should now be able to click the spinner and have your selected team displayed in cell C2.

By now, you should have a good idea of how to create a spinner with Excel's ActiveX controls. Let's delete the object we just created and make room for the new object we're about to create, although in this case, because of the spinner's nature, we're going to have to link the data to our cell using the INDEX formula. Although, for the purposes of this task, we're linking the spinner to text-based data, you can see that this control is more ideally suited to scrolling through a list of numbers.

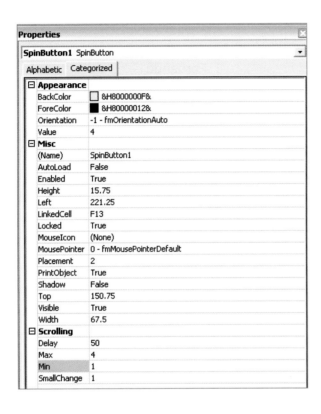

Properties

SpinButton1 SpinButton

Alphabetic | Categorized

⊟ **Appearance**	
BackColor	&H8000000F&
ForeColor	&H80000012&
Orientation	-1 - fmOrientationAuto
Value	4
⊟ **Misc**	
(Name)	SpinButton1
AutoLoad	False
Enabled	True
Height	15.75
Left	221.25
LinkedCell	F13
Locked	True
MouseIcon	(None)
MousePointer	0 - fmMousePointerDefault
Placement	2
PrintObject	True
Shadow	False
Top	150.75
Visible	True
Width	67.5
⊟ **Scrolling**	
Delay	50
Max	4
Min	1
SmallChange	1

3 Enter 4 as the Max, 1 as the Min, and 1 as the SmallChange, and, as with the form controls, you'll set the LinkedCell to something other than where you'll want your data displayed – in this case, to F14. Now, the final step is to insert the INDEX formula indicated above in cell C2, and you're all done.

4

Controls

=INDEX(J3:J6, F13, 0) ——————— 3

D	E	F	G

Adding a scroll bar

Now we're going to use the same procedure to add a scroll bar to the spreadsheet, first using the form controls, and then using the ActiveX controls. We'll use this tool for the Score column.

1 Click **Insert** on the Developer tab, and choose Scroll Bar. Draw your object below the other objects we've added as indicated in the image to the right.

2 Right-click the **image** and select Format Control from the dialogue. On the Control tab, make sure that the minimum value is 0 and the maximum value is 20. If this were another column, say for Team, where the data is text-based, we'd have to add another INSERT formula. But, conveniently enough, all we need is a list of numbers. So we can have the linked cell also be the one in which we want our data to display, cell D2.

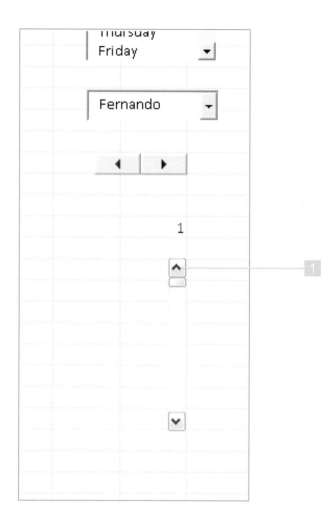

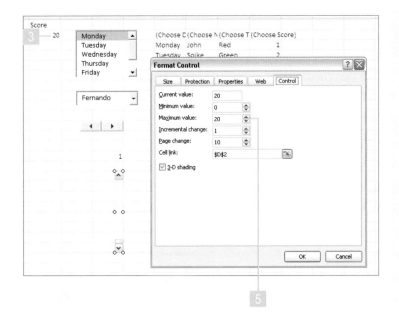

Adding a
scroll bar (cont.)

3 Click on your **scroll bar**, and you should be able to scroll between the possible scores while displaying your selection in cell D2.

Once again, we'll delete our object so we can re-create it using ActiveX controls.

4 Go to the Controls, click **Insert**, choose Scroll Bar from the ActiveX controls, and draw your object right where the previous scroll bar was.

5 Right-click on the object and select Properties. Now, set Max to 20 and Min to 1, with the LinkedCell set to D2.

6 When you close the Properties dialogue, you should be able to scroll through the scroll bar as your selection is displayed in cell D2. Once again, no INDEX formula is necessary.

Using OFFSET and scroll link in scroll bars

To illustrate how OFFSET can be used in conjunction with linking to a scroll bar, I've devised a brief scenario that I will apply to our fictional scorecard for our fictional game. Let's say that two games were supposed to be played, but one was rained out. Instead, everyone's score just gets multiplied by 1.5. (This is a fictional scenario, remember!) Now, say you want to link the revised score to a different cell in the spreadsheet and do the conversion on the fly. This is where using the OFFSET formula comes into play. This feature can prove very useful when working with enormous spreadsheets where excessive scrolling could stymie your workflow.

1 Enter the following formula into cell D13:

```
=(OFFSET(D2,0,0,1,1))*1.5
```

This formula references the cell D2, which is linked to the scroll bar, and, by having the row and column offset by 0 cells and 0 cells, respectively, it is displaying the result in the same cell where the formula has been entered. The final digits in the formula, in this case both set to 1, indicate how tall and how wide your resulting cell will be. Finally, we are multiplying the linked result data by 1.5.

2 Now type REVISED SCORE in cell B13 to make it clear to users what the number in D13 refers to. When you scroll through the list, cell D13 should display the number linked to cell D2 by 1.5. In the image, you will see that the score in D2 is 7, while the revised score in D13 is 10.5.

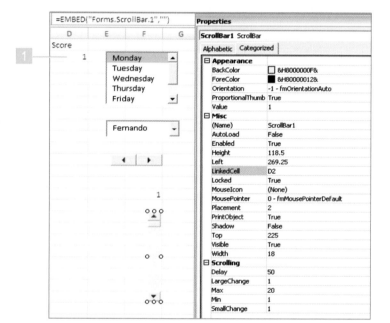

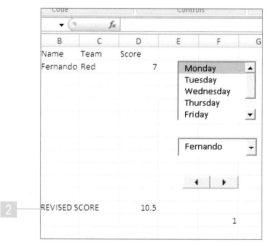

Now that you've seen how convenient and accessible form controls can make your spreadsheet, you might be interested in customising these interactive elements even more. With limited knowledge of Visual Basic for Applications (VBA), you can do just that. In this chapter, we will show you how to set up a user form, and where to find the tools you'll need. We will not, however, go into much depth as far as VBA coding is concerned. For more information on VBA coding, refer to Chapter 11 of this book, or check out the many websites available with free and easy-to-use tutorials, including the following URL, which focuses specifically on learning VBA for Excel applications: **http://www.excel-vba.com/excel-vba-contents.htm**

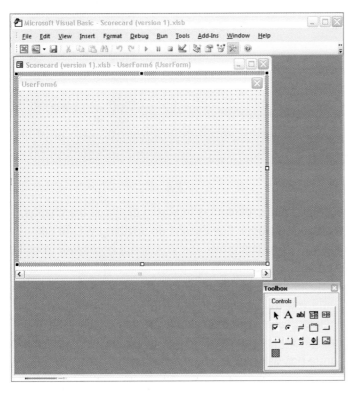

Creating a blank user form

1 To create a new user form, you'll need to go into the VBA editor, which is located on the Developer tab in the Code group, and click on **Visual Basic**.

2 Once in the VBA editor, click on the **Insert** button, and choose User Form. A new user form will appear along with a separate dialogue for the Toolbox. Note that the Controls found in the Toolbox are essentially the same as the ActiveX controls.

4

Creating a custom dialogue box

It is really quite easy to create a custom dialogue box, especially if you are already familiar with VBA scripting. Even if you're not familiar with VBA scripting, it is easy to set up the form itself, although it won't do anything until you add some code. Therefore, this chapter will walk you through the preliminary steps of setting up a custom dialogue box, but you may not get much use out of it until you've gone through Chapter 11 and familiarised yourself with VBA scripting.

It's time to get creative! Follow the steps laid out here and you should end up with a custom dialogue box similar to the one pictured below:

1 First, choose the Frame tool, indicated by a box with the letters XYZ marked on it. Draw a frame on the left-hand side of the UserForm.

2 Now, choose the ListBox tool, and use it to draw a list box inside the frame you created.

3 I've added a combo box on the upper right-hand side, and three text boxes (indicated on the Toolbox by the symbol, **ab|**).

4 Finally, I've added a place to put an image at the bottom right.

5 Now it's time to see what your custom dialogue box will look like in the spreadsheet interface. Click the **Run** button in the toolbar, and you will see your custom dialogue box appear in the spreadsheet like any other form.

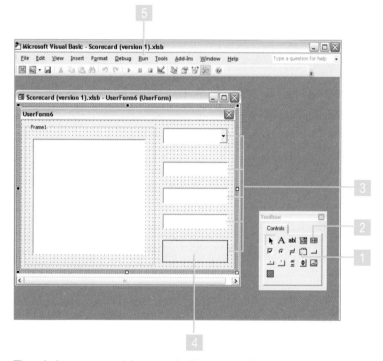

There's just one problem: as indicated earlier in the chapter, this custom dialogue box doesn't do anything yet. To see where you go to customise the VBA script necessary to make this creation more than just a pretty face, right-click on any of the objects drawn in the user form. Select View Code from the list, and you will be taken to the VBA script interface. As you can see on page 81, the only code present dictates the existence of the form itself. To add functionality to your custom dialogue box will require some scripting.

Creating a custom dialogue box (cont.)

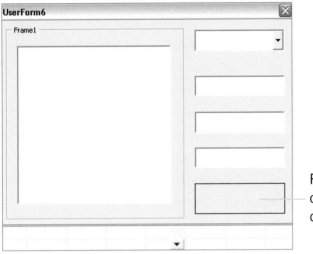

Right click an object

That will have to wait, however, as VBA scripting is covered later in the book. Now, it's time to move on to Chapter 5, but we'll have plenty of time for more advanced topics. Once again, if learning VBA script is something you're interested in, the above-cited URL is a good place to start.

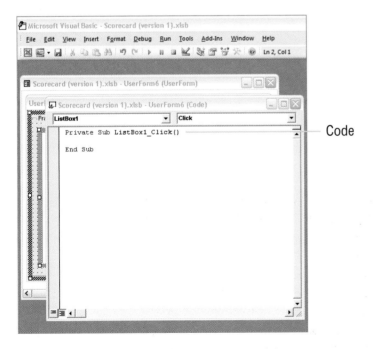

Code

PivotChart and PivotTable reports

Introduction

If you have a complex worksheet and you need to isolate a few key bits of data and compare them, PivotTable® and PivotChart® give you a great tool. PivotTable gathers the information for you on a separate sheet. With just a few clicks, you can substitute alternate data and compare it. You can then create a chart that visualises the data for you. PivotTable lets you apply filters and sort data in a way that allows you to create sophisticated reports.

In Excel 2007, PivotTable and PivotChart work differently compared to early versions of the application. But once you learn some tips about how to use them quickly, you'll use them more and more often.

Learning how PivotCharts and PivotTables present data

PivotTables simplify working with data because they instantly pick out data you want from a table and present it in a separate container. PivotTables can then quickly be turned into PivotCharts, which visually represent the data you have selected. Many of the tasks in this chapter will use a simple spreadsheet I created (with the help of my friend Polina Mesechcova) called PivotTableExample.xlsx, which you can download from the Pearson website **http://www.pearson.com**. Open the file in Excel 2007, and you can then try out your own simple PivotTable.

1 Select all the cells in the PivotTableExample file from A2 to I9.

2 Click the **Insert** tab.

3 Click **PivotTable**.

4 Choose PivotTable from the drop-down list.

5 Adjust the Table/Range information if needed.

6 Click **OK**.

A new PivotTable Tools menu, with the Options and Design tabs beneath it, appears at the top of the Excel window.

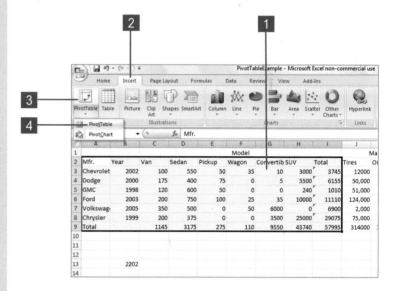

Learning how PivotCharts and PivotTables present data (cont.)

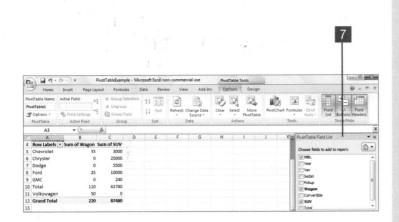

7 In the PivotTable Field List, which appears as a separate pane within the Excel window, check the boxes next to the fields you want to include in the PivotTable. Each time you check a box, an item is added to the table.

Did you know?

To make the PivotTable Field List reappear if you have closed it, click anywhere in the PivotTable itself. To delete a PivotTable, click **Options**, click the **Select** button, click **Entire PivotTable**, and press the [Delete] key.

5

Creating a PivotChart

Once you have created a PivotTable, it's a matter of a few mouse clicks to create a PivotChart. A PivotChart presents the same information as a PivotTable, but in a visual way – in the form of a graph or other graphic indicator. Excel gives you nearly 75 different options for how to lay out your chart, too. You don't have to create a PivotTable in order to assemble a PivotChart, either – you can click the PivotChart button to begin with and never have a table at all, if you want. This example, however, assumes that you already have a PivotTable in place.

1 Select the PivotTable.

2 Click **PivotChart** in the Tools group.

3 Click one of the general PivotChart types on the left side of the PivotChart dialogue box.

The available options are selected; they jump to the middle of the dialogue box if they aren't visible already.

4 Click the option you want.

5 Click **OK**.

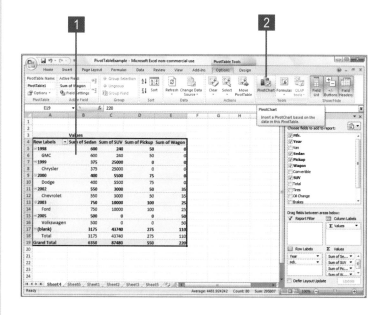

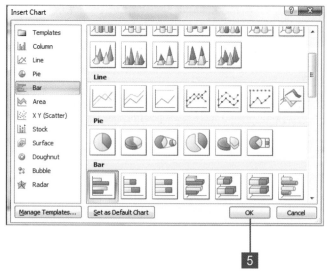

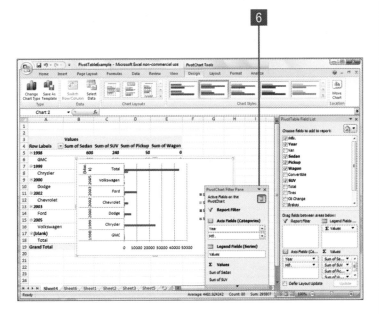

6 Click the **drop-down list** in the PivotChart Filter Pane to adjust the data in the chart if needed.

7 Click and drag the **chart** to reposition it.

8 Click the **chart's corners** to resize it so you can view other data.

For your information

You can create a PivotTable from virtually any worksheet. But they are ideally suited to complex and lengthy spreadsheets with many different types of data. Whenever you need to save time by getting a quick look at data and comparing one type of information to another, a PivotTable is an ideal tool.

5

Manually filtering data for a PivotTable report

PivotTables are selections of the data contained in a more extensive worksheet. But if the worksheet is extensive, the PivotTable can grow dramatically in size and complexity, too. You can filter the data you want displayed in the PivotTable by writing a query. But an easy way is to select your own filters by choosing from Excel's built-in controls. You can filter the data either before or after the PivotTable is created. You can create three types: manual, label or value filters.

1 Right-click any field in the PivotTable.

2 Point to Filter.

3 Choose either Keep Only Selected Items (if you want to delete all other fields except the ones you have currently selected) or Hide Selected Items (which filters out the selected fields).

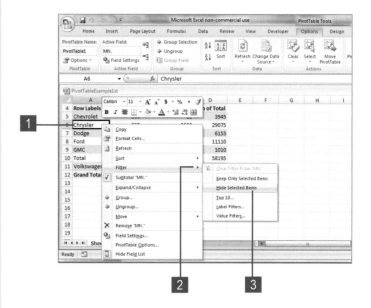

For your information

The values contained in a PivotTable report can't be manually filtered. When you right-click individual values, you don't see the Filter option in the context menu. Any other part of the report can be filtered in this way, however.

Label filters give you a finer-grained level of control over the data that appears in a PivotTable than you can get with manual filters. Some of the control comes from the way labels are designated: you can tell Excel to filter data based on a string or a numeric component, in addition to a variety of other operators. To create this sort of filter, you open the Label Filter dialogue box using one of three options. Then you choose from a list of operators.

Filtering PivotTable labels

1 Do one of the following:

a Right-click one of the items listed in either the Column Labels or Row Labels section of the Report Layout area at the bottom of the Pivot Table Field List pane. Mouse over Filter and choose Label Filters.

b Mouse over one of the fields in the fields area of the PivotTable Field List pane. Choose Label Filters from the dialogue box that appears.

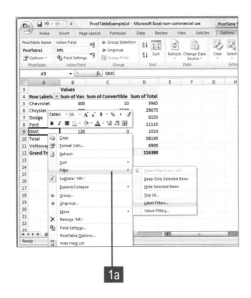

1a

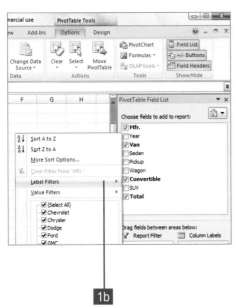

1b

Filtering PivotTable labels (cont.)

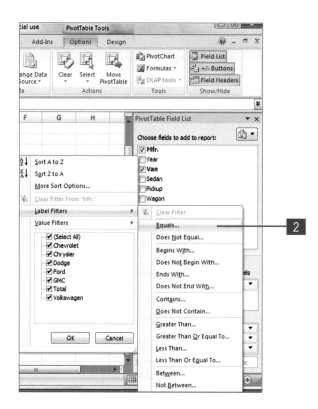

2 In either case, you access a selection of filtering options. They are seen clearly if you choose option 1b above, mouse over Label Filters, and access the submenu. Choose the filter you want to apply to the selected field.

3 When the Label Filter dialogue box appears, type the filter criteria in the box on the right.

4 Click **OK**.

The Label Filter operators and explanations of what they do are shown in Table 5.1.

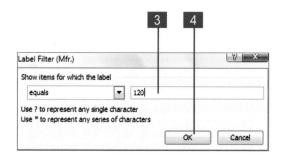

Did you know?

You can refine the way Excel filters PivotTable data by implementing special operators called wildcards. Wildcards like the question mark (?) represent a single character. The asterisk (*) stands for a group of characters. For example, typing F* in the Filter Value field and choosing the Begins With operator will turn up all words beginning with the letter F.

Table 5.1 Label filter operators

Operator	What it does
Equals	Displays data that is equal to the contents of the Filter Value field
Does Not Equal	Displays data that is not equal to the number or text in the Filter Value field
Begins with	Displays data that begins with the characters shown in the Filter Value field
Does Not Begin With	Displays data that does not begin with the characters shown in the Filter Value field
Is Greater Than	Displays data that is greater than the characters shown in the Filter Value field
Is Greater Than or Equal To	Displays data that is less than or equal to the characters shown in the Filter Value field
Is Less Than	Displays data that is less than the characters shown in the Filter Value field
Is Less Than or Equal To	Displays data that is less than or equal to the characters shown in the Filter Value field
Begins With	Displays data that begins with the same characters shown in the Filter Value field
Does Not Begin With	Displays data that does not begin with the characters shown in the Filter Value field
Ends With	Displays data that ends with text specified in the Filter Value field
Does Not End With	Displays any data that does not end with thetext specified in the Filter Value field
Contains	Displays data that contains the characters shown in the Filter Value field
Does Not Contain	Displays any data that does not contain the characters shown in the Filter Value field
Is Between	Displays data that is contained between text or numerals shown in the first and last Filter Value fields
Is Not Between	Displays any data that is not between the text or numerals shown in the first and last Filter Value fields

5

Creating value filters

If you need to create reports that gather specific sums or figures that fall within a specific numeric range, value filters are the perfect option. Value filters let you narrow in on results so that you can present to decision makers the figures they want to know about.

1 Do one of the following:

a Right-click any row or column label in your PivotTable, point to Filter, and choose Value Filters from the context menu.

b Mouse over one of the fields in the PivotTable Field List pane, click the **down arrow**, and choose Value Filters from the drop-down menu.

In either case, the Value Filters dialogue box options appear. If you choose option 1b, they appear as a submenu. If you choose 1b, you see the Value Filters dialogue box shown here.

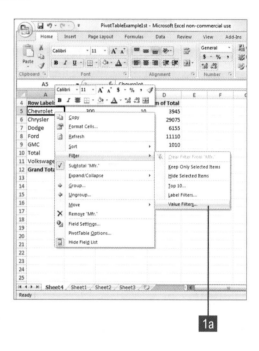

1a

1b

Choose a field.

Choose a value filter operator.

Type in characters or numerals.

Click **OK**.

The filter criteria are applied and the filtered data are presented.

	A	B	C	D
4	Row Labels	Sum of Van	Sum of Convertible	Sum of Total
5	Total	1345	9550	58195
6	**Grand Total**	**1345**	**9550**	**58195**

Did you know?

Label fields and value fields are new to Excel 2007.

Styling a PivotTable report

Most of a report's impact comes from the data within it. But if the report is difficult to read or formatted poorly, part of that impact is diluted. Once you have selected the data you want to include in your PivotTable, give some thought to how the table itself is styled. You don't need to stay with the default look and feel of the presentation, but can choose one of a variety of design and formatting options.

1 Click the **Design** tab under PivotTable tools.

2 Select the PivotTable to make the design tools active.

3 Mouse over each of the styles to choose one.

4 Scroll through the list to see more options.

5 Click here to choose banded rows and/or banded columns.

Setting a default style

1 Right-click the style you are currently using in the PivotTable Styles group.

2 Choose Set As Default from the context menu.

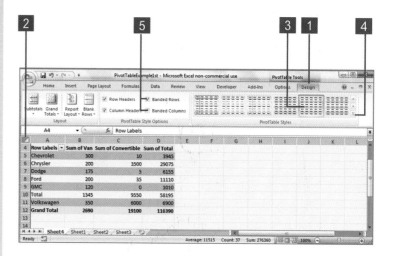

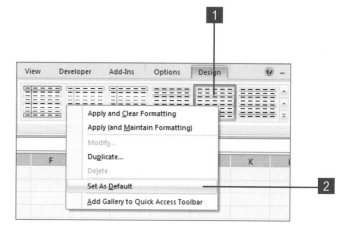

In addition to the colours and styles of the PivotTable, you can adjust the layout of the table. The layout includes field labels, column headings, buttons and subtotals. You have three layout options from which to choose.

You find these three options by clicking the **Report Layout** button in the Layout group in the Design tab. Make sure you select the PivotTable in order to display the Design tab.

Compact

This is the default layout. Field labels are shown instead of field headings. All of the fields in the Row Labels area are merged into one column.

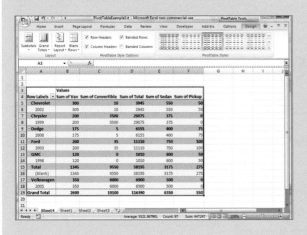

Outline

In outline layout, field headings are displayed instead of field labels. Each field in the Row Labels area is shown in an individual column.

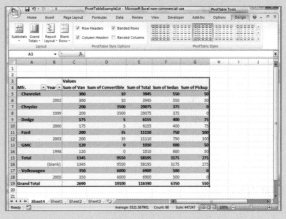

Tabular

In tabular layout, field headings are shown, subtotals are displayed on a subtotal line at the bottom of each group, and each field in the Row Labels area has its own column. A grid is shown in the background.

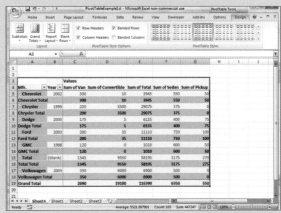

5

Adjusting PivotTable options

Hide or show options

1 Click **Options**.

2 Click the **Field List** button to toggle the display of the Field List.

3 Click here to show/hide the group buttons.

4 Click here to show or hide field headers for columns or rows.

Access more PivotTable options

5 Click **PivotTable**.

6 Click **Options**.

Many of the features described so far in this chapter are useful. But how do you remove or adjust them? For instance, if you're used to working in Excel 2003 or earlier versions, it takes some time to figure out how to use the Field List that appears (by default) on the right side of the Excel window when a PivotTable is selected. You can make it visible or invisible, group data, select elements and clear filters and other formatting by using the Options tab, which appears under PivotTable Tools when the PivotTable is selected.

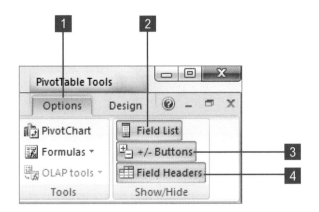

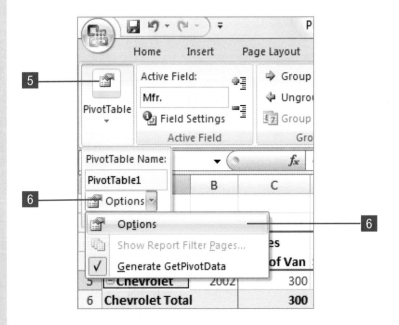

7 Change the name of the PivotTable here.

8 Change the format of the PivotTable here.

9 Toggle the display of grand totals and related options here.

10 Change the way the data is sorted and related options here.

11 Decide whether to print buttons, row labels, and set print titles here.

12 Save source data and related options here.

13 Click **OK**.

5

Refreshing PivotTable report data

In order to analyse data, you have to make sure it's up to date. Before you draw conclusions, you might want to refresh the data that is currently displayed.

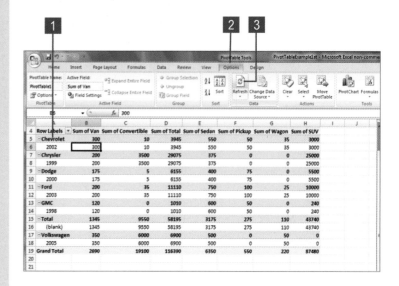

1 Click anywhere in the PivotTable report.

2 Click the **Options** tab.

3 Click **Refresh**.

Did you know?

You can do this for either PivotTables or PivotCharts; the steps are almost the same. For PivotCharts click the **chart**, click the **Analyze** tab, and click the **Refresh** button.

PivotTable contents are by their nature complex. They have been culled from larger worksheets that are often complex and lengthy. By charting a PivotTable, you give others an overview of the contents and an easy way to draw conclusions because the information is presented visually. When you create a PivotChart, a new tab called Analyze appears. It contains controls for collapsing or expanding fields, refreshing or clearing data, and showing or hiding features such as the Field List.

Creating a PivotChart report from a PivotTable report

---

1. Click anywhere in the PivotTable.

2. Click the **Options** tab.

3. Click **PivotChart**.

4. Choose the layout option you want.

5. Click **OK**.

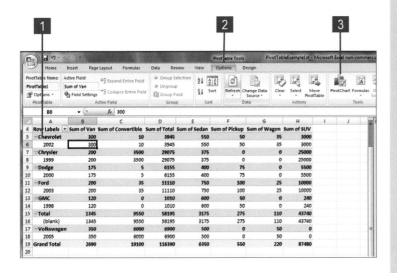

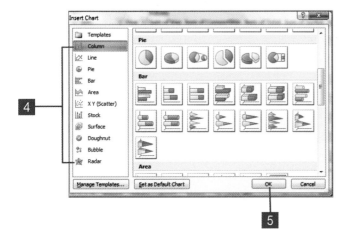

Creating a PivotChart report from a PivotTable report (cont.)

The PivotChart appears along with the PivotChart Filter Pane; reposition them by dragging so you can view them clearly along with the PivotTable.

Layout tab

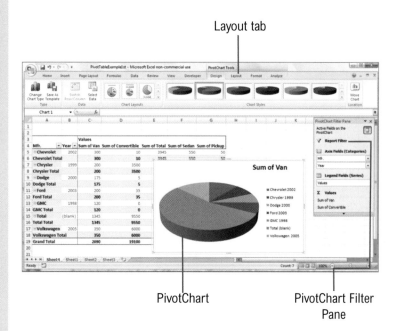

PivotChart

PivotChart Filter Pane

For your information

If you look at the PivotChart Filter Pane closely, you'll notice that nearly all of its functions are duplicated in the PivotTable Field List pane. So to save space on screen, you can close one or the other. This is particularly useful if you want to examine a PivotChart and PivotTable at the same time.

Even if you create a PivotChart from data presented in a PivotTable, the results aren't 'written in stone'. You can always adjust them to clarify your report. If you ever want to rename a report, just click the **Options** tab, type the new name in the PivotTable Name box, and press [Enter].

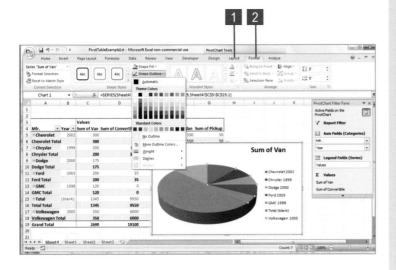

Changing a PivotChart's format

1 Click the **Layout** tab to adjust the PivotChart in much the same way you would edit any chart.

2 Click the **Format** tab to fill shapes and change type designs or other visual aspects of the chart.

3 Click the **Analyze** tab not to perform analysis on the data, but to refresh data, clear filters or change the active tab.

5

Formulas and functions in reports

Introduction

As you learned in the previous chapter, PivotTables are convenient and versatile, but they can be powerful calculation tools as well. Because of their versatility and convenience, when you do calculations with PivotTables by adding formulas and functions, you're instantly rewarded with handsome charts and data presentation that are almost infinitely customisable. You can also use tools more commonly seen in regular spreadsheets, such as iteration or AutoComplete, in new and robust ways.

One of the best ways to think about formulas and functions in PivotTables is in context of a year-end sales presentation. You have enormous amounts of data that you've organised into PivotTables, meaning they can be easily customised, but you'll need to make sense of it all. With formulas and functions in PivotTables, you can do everything from summarising data based on averages to displaying the relationship between different datasets. You can even use things like iteration in conjunction with PivotTables to calculate compound interest, for example. Moreover, the changes that Microsoft has implemented for Excel 2007 make this kind of operation easier than ever.

What you'll do

Add a formula to a report

Format data using custom formulas

Take advantage of formula AutoComplete

Sort text

Set up a simple iteration

Modify an aggregate function

Adding a formula to a report

Adding a formula to a report can give your report meaning and help you to glean potentially hidden data from it. Because of how versatile PivotTable reports are, you can run new formulas every time you customise, or 'pivot', your pivot table and draw new meaning out of it. This is especially helpful when you are going to do a presentation, for example, and you want to be able to analyse your data in multiple so as to impart a deeper understanding of it to your audience.

Create a PivotTable

1 For this task, enter the data you see in the adjacent image into a spreadsheet, or load the sample Formulas in Report, which you'll find on this book's website, and click **Sheet 1**.

2 Click the **Insert** tab.

3 Click **PivotTable** and insert a PivotTable into a new sheet.

4 Select the Quarter, Profits and Employee fields in the Pivot Table Field List as shown opposite.

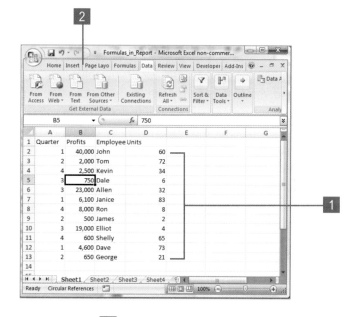

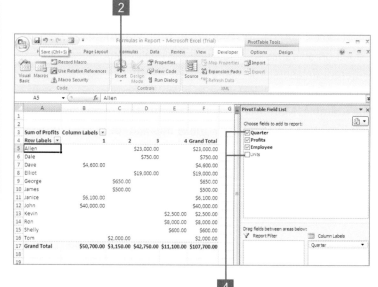

A PivotTable report will sum your data automatically, of course, but it can also do a lot more than that. The possibilities for analysing and presenting custom data reports is limited only by your imagination, and because you can keep adding new PivotTables, a complex and sophisticated report is only a few clicks away. Suppose you want to figure out what each employee's sales commission will be for this set of sales data, assuming they get 12 per cent of their sales in commissions.

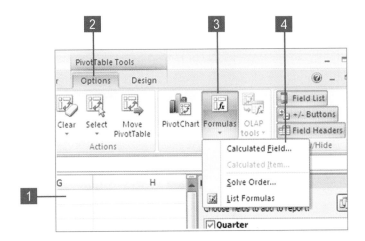

Add a Formula

1 Click anywhere in the PivotTable to make the PivotTables toolbar visible.

2 Click the **Options** tab under the PivotTable toolbar.

3 Click **Formulas**.

4 Select **Calculated Field** from the resulting drop-down menu.

Adding a formula to a report (cont.)

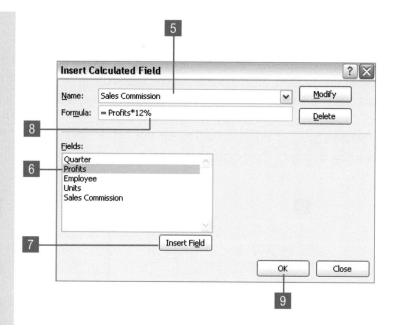

5 In the Insert Calculated Field dialogue that appears, type Sales Commission in the Name field.

6 In the Formula field, click **Profits** from the Fields list.

7 Click **Insert Field**.

8 Now, add *12% to complete the formula (operators are the same as in spreadsheets). Your dialogue box should look like the adjacent image.

9 Click **OK**.

10 Create a new PivotTable in a new worksheet: first, select the Pivot Table data.

11 Click **Insert**.

12 Click **PivotTable**, and choose PivotTable from the drop-down menu.

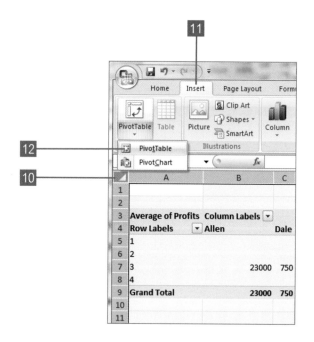

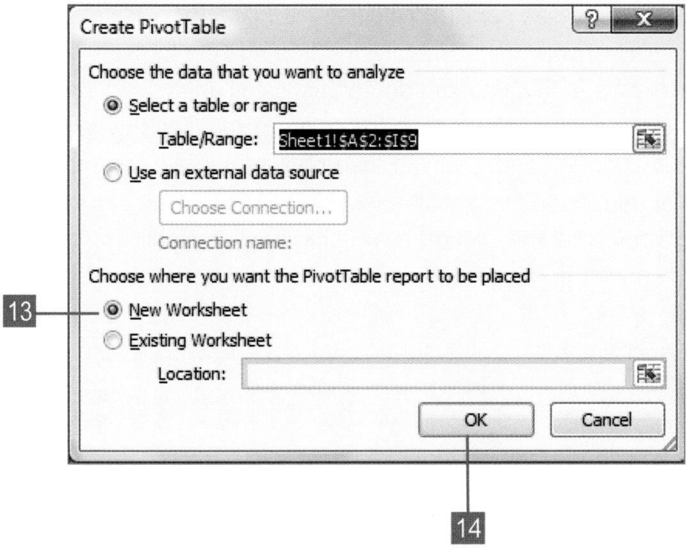

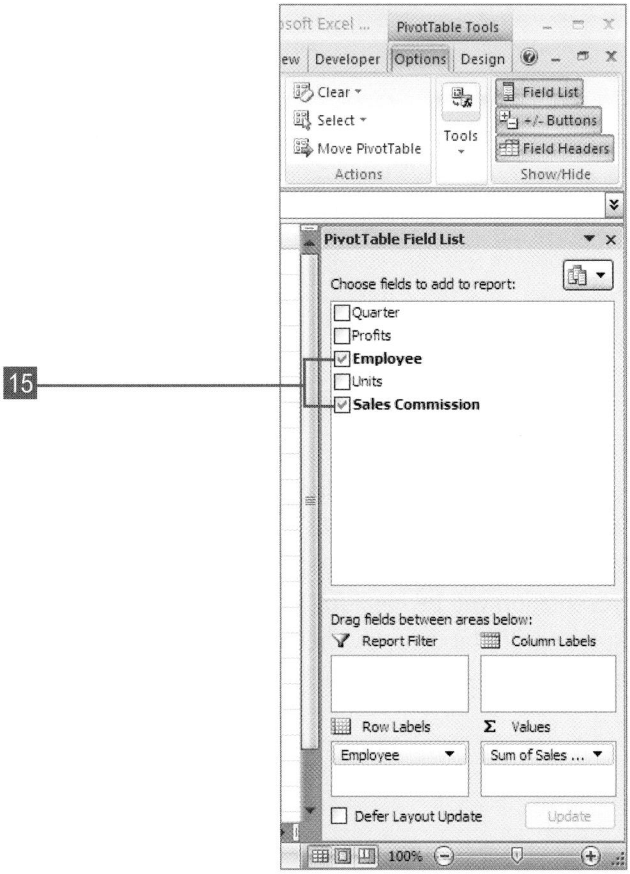

Create PivotTable

Choose the data that you want to analyze

● Select a table or range

    Table/Range: Sheet1!$A$2:$I$9

○ Use an external data source

    Choose Connection...

    Connection name:

Choose where you want the PivotTable report to be placed

13 ● New Worksheet

○ Existing Worksheet

    Location:

OK   Cancel

14

---

soft Excel ...   PivotTable Tools

ew | Developer | Options | Design

- Clear ▾
- Select ▾
- Move PivotTable
- Tools
- Field List
- +/- Buttons
- Field Headers

Actions   Show/Hide

PivotTable Field List

Choose fields to add to report:

☐ Quarter
☐ Profits
☑ **Employee**
☐ Units
☑ **Sales Commission**

15

Drag fields between areas below:

▼ Report Filter   Column Labels

Row Labels   Σ Values

Employee ▾   Sum of Sales ... ▾

☐ Defer Layout Update   Update

100%

Adding a formula to a report (cont.)

6

13 Make sure New Worksheet is selected.

14 Click **OK**.

15 Select Employee and your new field, Sales Commission, from the PivotTable Field List. The resulting report should look like the adjacent image.

Formatting data using custom formulas

Custom formulas perform calculations that let you really get to the heart of your data by analysing it in relation to itself. What this means is that you can do sophisticated analysis to draw out less obvious information from your data. With the new information in hand, you can then present it in a clear and easily understood way with a PivotTable report. You can see custom formulas in action by reusing the PivotTable you worked with in the preceding task.

1 Modify your PivotTable in the PivotTable Field List so that it corresponds to the adjacent image: select the Quarter, Profits and Employee fields.

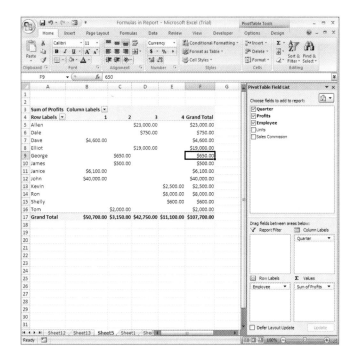

For this example, you're going to format the data using the Running Total in function. As you'll see, this will make your data table clearer, cleaner and easier to read. The resulting presentation will be ideal for a presentation to someone not as familiar with the data who benefits from a graceful and simple layout.

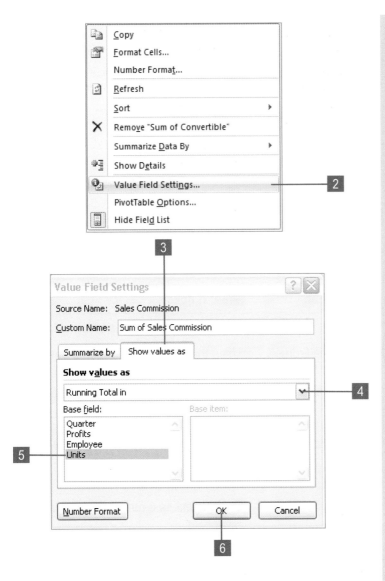

2 Right-click anywhere within the PivotTable data, and select Value Field Settings from the resulting context menu.

3 Click the **Show values as** tab.

4 Select Running Total in from the Show values as drop-down list.

5 Choose Units as your Base Field, so that the resulting report will show how many units each employee sold, and display only how much revenue was generated.

6 Click **OK**.

For your information

You cannot select something presented in your report as a sum of values, only something listed as a row or column label. On second thoughts, you *can*, but your settings will produce a meaningless table populated by pound signs.

Formatting data using custom formulas (cont.)

As you can see opposite, profits are now only listed for the Units rows, clearing up the report and making it easier to read. Table 6-1 lists the types of custom calculations you can perform on your PivotTable data.

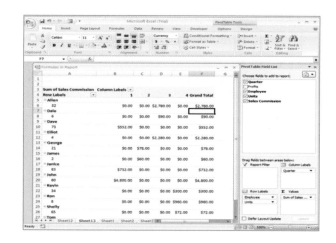

Table 6.1 Custom calculations

Calculation	What it does
Normal	Summarises the Values area field
Difference From	Uses the difference between a base and field item to summarise data
% Of	Uses the percentage of a base field item to summarise data
% Difference From	Uses the percentage of difference between a base and field item to summarise data
Running Total in	Shows data as a running total in a base field
% Of Row	Uses the percentage of total row value to display data
% Of Column	Uses the percentage of total column value to display data
% Total	Uses percentage of the total value from the report to display data
Index	Uses the formula: `((Cell Value)*(Grand Total of Grand Totals))/((Grand Row Total)*(Grand Column Total)).`

Formula AutoComplete is a very useful tool when working in spreadsheets alone, but it can also facilitate PivotTable analysis. For all the flexibility and convenience of calculations and data sorting from within PivotTable reports, you may want to get some calculations done in the spreadsheet itself, adjacent to the report. In this case, you're likely to find the AutoComplete feature very useful indeed. In this next exercise, you're going to take advantage of the AutoComplete function to facilitate calculating the average sales per quarter.

Taking advantage of formula AutoComplete

6

1 Create a PivotTable report like the one pictured here. It will include the fields Quarter, Profits and Employee.

2 Next you'll insert a function in the cells next to your PivotTable. Insert the function into Column I so you have enough room to label the information for the benefit of your viewers. Click on the cell where you want to insert the function, and hit the [=] sign.

3 Type the letter 'a', and a list of formulas will appear in a drop-down menu.

4 Choose AVERAGE.

5 Notice the information caption that describes what this particular function does.

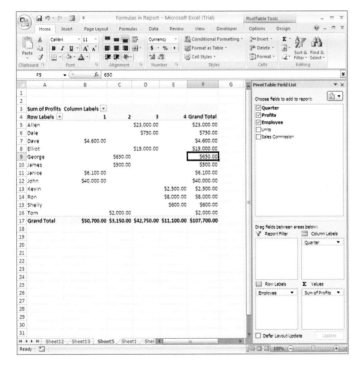

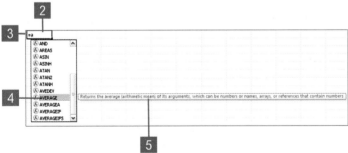

Taking advantage of formula AutoComplete (cont.)

6 Now we're going to fill in the fields. Click in the parentheses following the word AVERAGE and select the values in Quarter 1, 2, 3 and 4, respectively.

7 If you're not sure exactly what you're supposed to do, or where you are in the formula, just look to the caption that automatically appears as a reminder.

8 Finally, enter the text, 'QUARTER', 'AVERAGE SALES', the numbers, '1', '2', '3' and '4' as shown to complete your external data analysis.

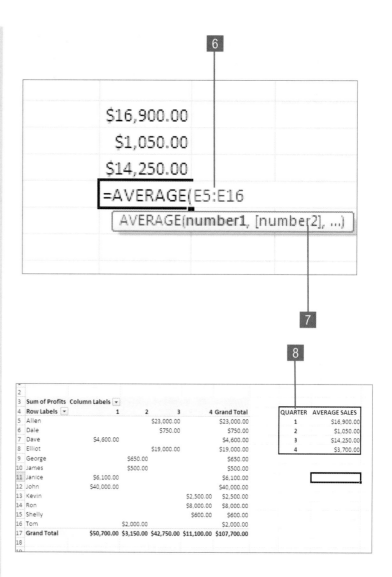

Did you know?

AutoComplete in Excel 2007 has applications in the creation and analysis of CUBE functions in association with Online Analytical Processing (OLAP), which requires linking to external databases. This is commonly, but not exclusively, accomplished through MySQL Server, and is beyond the scope of this book. For more information, visit: **http://office.microsoft.com/en-us/excel/CH100648531033.aspx**

Sorting is always a useful way to organise information so that it's easier to interpret. Microsoft has made it easy to sort text in PivotTable reports. Just leave the report that you have been working with open, and follow these steps.

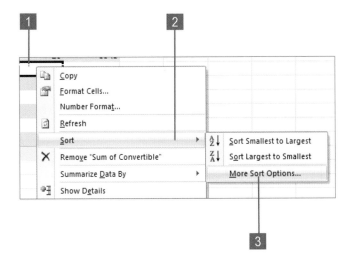

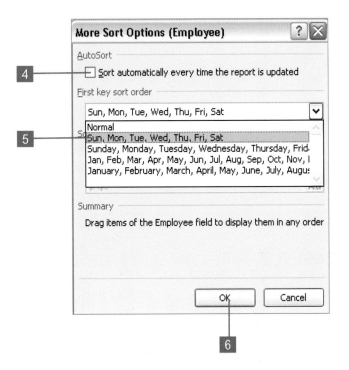

1 To sort the text, right-click on any name in the list of employees (that's all the text we have in this particular case).

2 Point to **Sort**.

3 Click **More Sort Options**.

4 Here you can choose how often you would like the sort performed, or check the box next to sort automatically every time the report is updated.

5 Choose the days of the week from the First key sort order drop-down menu.

6 Click **OK**.

Sorting text (cont.)

7 When you go back to the previous dialogue, choose Ascending by Employee (in the drop-down menu). Click **OK**, and your employees should now be alphabetised.

Sum of Profits	Column Labels ▾				
Row Labels ▾	1	2	3	4	Grand Total
Allen		$23,000.00			$23,000.00
Dale		$750.00			$750.00
Dave	$4,600.00				$4,600.00
Elliot		$19,000.00			$19,000.00
George			$650.00		$650.00
James			$500.00		$500.00
Janice	$6,100.00				$6,100.00
John	$40,000.00				$40,000.00
Kevin				$2,500.00	$2,500.00
Ron				$8,000.00	$8,000.00
Shelly				$600.00	$600.00
Tom			$2,000.00		$2,000.00
Grand Total	$50,700.00	$3,150.00	$42,750.00	$11,100.00	$107,700.00

7

To understand simple iteration is to gain insight into a very fundamental element of programming more generally, because it's an example of recursive logic. When you calculate values, you enable Excel to perform an operation that is self-referential. Iteration in Excel is most commonly used to compound interest, because this is a case-in-point example of a calculation that must inherently refer to itself. It might seem a little complicated at first, but understanding the subtleties of iteration inherently requires that you understand *why* you're using it and what you're using it for. At the very least, this task will show you how to enable iterative calculation and give you an example of how it's done.

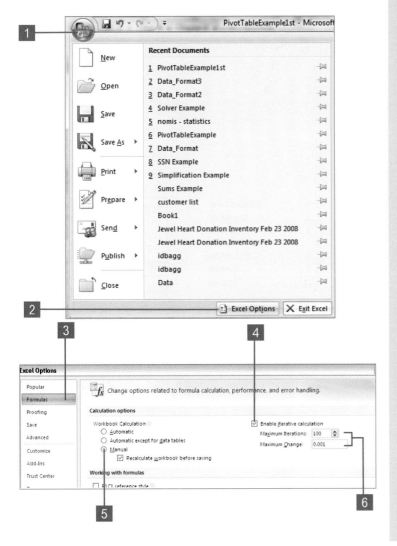

Enable iterative calculation

1 To enable iterative calculation, click on the **Office** button.

2 Choose Excel Options.

3 Click on **Formulas**.

4 Check the box next to Enable iterative calculation.

5 Select the Manual calculation option.

6 Choose 100 Maximum iterations and .001 Maximum change. What this does is delimit the amount of change that your iteration causes. In other words, since it is self-referential, the change becomes smaller and smaller each time. By the time you've gone through five or six iterations, the change is often going to be negligible. Likewise, by the time the change is only reflected in the thousands place, it's probably not necessary to continue iterating.

Formulas and functions in reports 111

Setting up a simple iteration (cont.)

7 In cell I10, enter the following formula:

```
=I10*I11
```

In cell I11, enter the following formula:

```
=H11*I19
```

In cell I14, enter the following formula:

```
=IF(RESET,0,
(I12*H11))
```

In H19, enter the following formula:

```
=IF(RESET,0,H18+
H19)
```

In I19, enter the following formula:

```
=IF(H19>I16,I1,
IF(RESET,I12,
I19+I11 ))
```

8 Now, click in cell H12 and click **F3** to access the Name Manager, and click **New**. In the Name field, type RESET.

9 Click **OK**, and then **Close** in the Name Manager window. This step is necessary in that it allows you to reset the iteration and bring it back to zero. Otherwise, after the first calculation was effected, you would be stuck with those results forever.

Set up an iterative calculation

You're going to set up an iterative calculation that determines how much actual profit is reflected by the sales figures if the funds are going into an account that earns 5 per cent interest after being compounded ten times (this assumes that the sales figures represent profit). To do this, you will first need to enter the interest rate, .05, in a cell. So you can have your interest calculator right next to the PivotTable, choose cell H11 for this value. You'll put whatever value on which you want to compound interest in cell I12, so now you'll have to enter some formulas to make it all work.

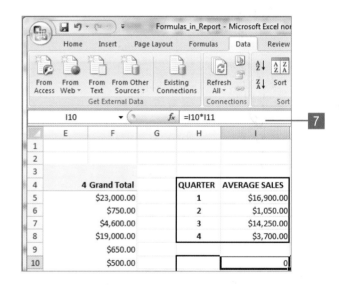

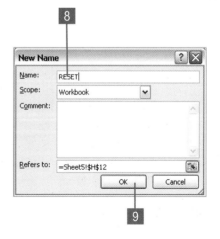

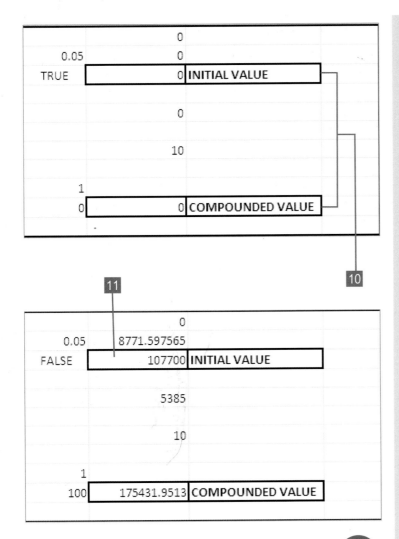

10 Now, format the region of your spreadsheet as seen in the opposite, adding the text INITIAL VALUE and COMPOUNDED VALUE as indicated. Cell I16 serves the purpose of halting the recursion process after ten iterations.

11 Now for the fascinating part. If you've entered the formulas correctly, Excel should provide you with the compounded value in the appropriate field. Enter the Grand Total from the PivotTable, $107,700.00, into cell I13. Make sure that FALSE is entered in cell I12 and hit [F9] to run the calculation.

For your information

You now know that the Grand Total of your sales figures, compounded ten times, produces $175,431.95. If you want to compound it further, just change the value in I16. You will notice that, if you continue to run the calculation by hitting [F9], the value in H19 will continuously increase. This is because your formula is still running iterations, but because you have blocked any change after ten iterations, the calculations are not reflected in your result. Finally, remember that you can reset your iteration by typing TRUE in cell H12, and then hitting [F9].

Modifying an aggregate function

Modifying the aggregate function is similar to creating a custom calculation, and is very simple to accomplish. You may have noticed that, when you create a PivotTable, the default setting for the values field is SUM. Excel lets you compare your data in many different ways, however, and this is where the aggregate function modification comes into play. Instead of having the data displayed as a sum of profits, you're going to display the average of profits per quarter.

1 Use the spreadsheet you created for this chapter, and create a new PivotTable following the adjacent image.

2 Right-click anywhere in the dataset, and choose Value Field Settings, much as you did when you created a custom formula earlier in this chapter. But this time, choose the Summarize by tab.

3 Select Average.

4 Click **OK**.

5 You can now see the profits summarised as an average. The average profits per quarter are at $8,975. You can see how easy it would be to summarise by any criteria that interested you.

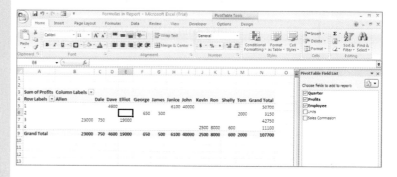

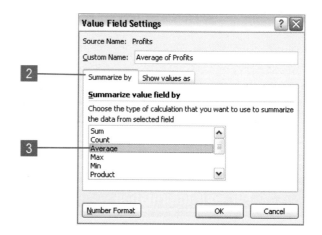

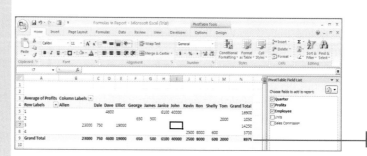

Tables and charts in reports

Introduction

Security is a major concern when working with financial records or other data in Excel. You need to be able to manage which content is displayed and which is blocked. You also need to protect your data by locking it so unauthorized users cannot alter it. And you need to protect yourself from viruses and other harmful software that infect macros. In previous versions of Excel, security was managed by means of prompts to the user. In Excel 2007, security has been automated to some extent. In addition, features like encryption and digital signatures have been integrated into the program in a streamlined way. This chapter describes some simple tasks you can take to make working with data in Excel safe, and to control how the program manages security.

What you'll do

Create a spreadsheet report

Sort spreadsheet report data

Rearrange report columns

Automatically refresh report data

Use conditional formatting with reports

Use charts to find business intelligence

Apply picture and texture fills

Combine chart types

Modify PivotCharts

Creating a spreadsheet report

To create a spreadsheet report, you'll call upon the knowledge gained in Chapter 3 by first importing the data that you are going to render into a spreadsheet report. As you may remember, there are many sources from which you can import data. But for this task, you'll import data from another Excel file for the sake of simplicity; in fact, this first section will be more of a review than anything else. You're going to use the spreadsheet that you created by importing data from the US Census Bureau's website in Chapter 2.

1 Click the **Data** tab.

2 Click **Get External Data**.

3 Choose From Microsoft Query.

4 Click **Browse** and browse to the file entitled Housing Price Data that should be saved somewhere on your hard drive.

5 When Microsoft Query automatically opens, it will ask if you want to Add Tables. Go to Options and make sure that every box is checked.

6 Click **OK**.

7 Click **Add** to add the table to your query.

8 Now go ahead and check every item in Table Options. Having more tables will better illustrate how spreadsheet reports can make life easier by helping you to manage large amounts of data.

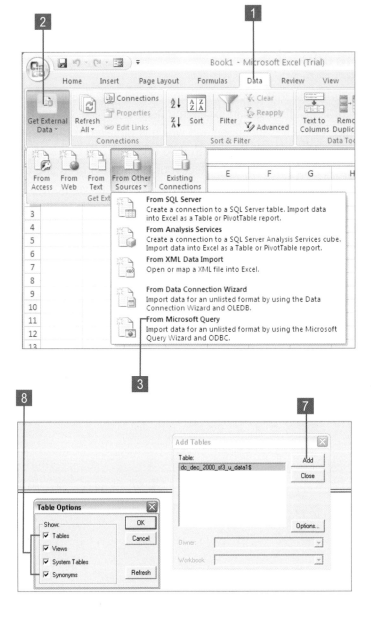

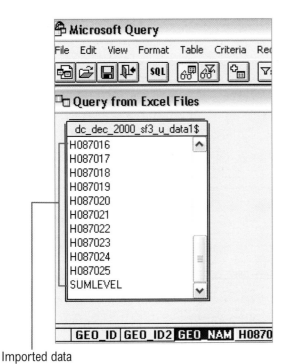

Imported data

Creating a spreadsheet report (cont.)

7

9 Click the **Close** box to exit the query.

10 When asked how you want to import the data, choose Table.

11 Click **OK**.

Creating a spreadsheet report (cont.)

12 Excel will pre-select a table template for you, but you can always change it by going to the Table Styles group in the Design tab. You don't have to choose the one that I have selected, but this is the style that you'll be seeing in the examples from here on out. Also, the Table Tools should now be enabled.

You'll notice that some of the fields in Row 2 are blank. It's important to note that contingencies like this are often encountered when importing data, even from an Excel file. Luckily, in this case, it's an easy fix because you already have the spreadsheet that you imported the data from.

13 Open the actual file entitled Housing Price Data, and select Row 2.

14 Now go to your spreadsheet report, select Row 2, and paste the data you just copied. If you get the warning that the data on the clipboard is not the same size and shape as the selected area, just click **OK** to continue.

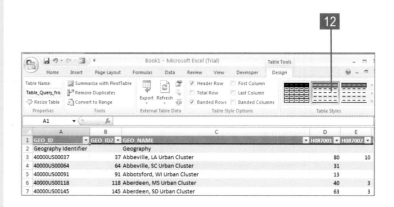

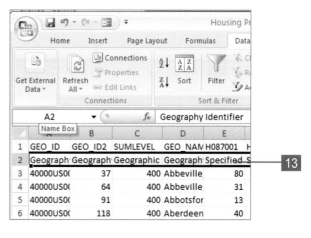

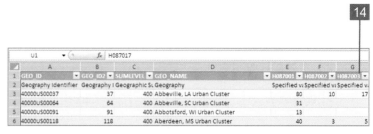

15 Your columns most likely won't be of uniform width, so go to the Cells group in the Home tab, and click **Format**. Select a column width of 10.

16 Click **OK**.

7

Sorting spreadsheet report data

Sorting data in a spreadsheet report is a powerful way to manipulate the information you have so that it tells you exactly what you want to know. Excel 2007 provides several easily accessible ways to sort your data, and if you don't find one that conforms exactly to what you're looking for, you can always create a custom list. There are two primary ways of sorting your data.

1 Click the **Home** tab.

2 Click the controls in the editing group under the Home tab.

3 Another way is by clicking on the dropdown that was automatically created in your Column headers when you created the spreadsheet report.

The way data is sorted depends largely on the type of data that you have selected. Some common sorting possibilities include:

■ Sorting text.

■ Sorting numbers.

■ Sorting dates or times.

■ Sorting by conditional formatting – this means that you have chosen to apply a certain colour, icon or font to cells containing values that meet certain conditions, such as exceeding a particular value, for example. This will be discussed later in the chapter.

■ Sorting by rows or columns.

■ Sorting by a custom list.

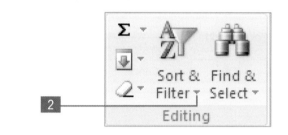

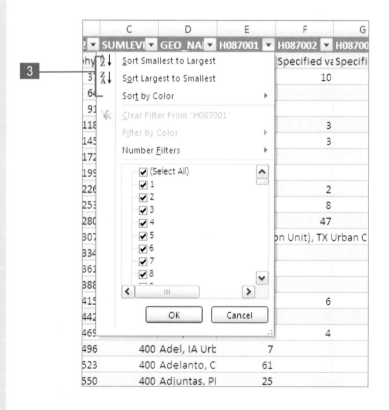

In this task, you'll see sorting put into practice and go through the basic steps that each of these types of sorting involves. Let's say you're interested in buying a home that falls within the $125,000 to $149,000 range. That information is stored within column T, but the report is currently organised alphabetically by geographic region, and you're not going to go through every column one by one to see where the most housing units are located. Sorting is the easy solution.

4 Click on the drop-down menu under the header for column T, and select Number Filters. As you can see, Top 10 is one sorting option. This would be a good way to get a broad initial sense of what regions you may want to look into.

5 Choose Top in the left-hand field, 10 in the centre field, and Items in the field on the right.

6 Click **OK**.

7 Now your report displays only the top ten results in your category. To get a better view, drag column T over to column D so you can compare the numbers directly to their respective geographic regions.

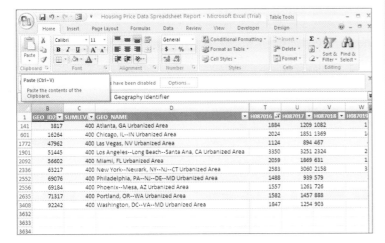

Now you can easily see that Los Angeles, New York and Chicago have the highest number of for-sale housing units. Note also that the filter symbol has appeared in column T, indicating that this column is sorted. You can easily remove your filter by clicking on the filter icon and choosing Remove filter from the resulting menu. You can get more information on sorting and filtering from the following website:
http://office.microsoft.com/en-us/excel/HP102245021033.aspx

Rearranging report columns

Sometimes, you find yourself looking at a spreadsheet, when you realise that it would make more sense for the columns to be where the rows are and vice versa. Excel 2007 provides an easy and straightforward way to rearrange columns or rows in a spreadsheet report. In this next example, you'll take a portion of the spreadsheet report you've created and rearrange it so that the name of the geographic region constitutes the column header and the housing unit price increment constitutes the row.

1 For starters, remove the filter from your spreadsheet report, so you can work with it in its unaltered form.

2 Now, select the data from column D through H, and row 1 through 10, delineating a portion of the report with data for the areas of Abbeville, LA, to Abernathy, TX, and for housing from $0 to $19,999. Remember, you can do this by clicking on the **Copy** icon in the Clipboard group on the Home tab, or you can simply hit [Ctrl]+[C].

3 To rearrange your columns to rows, you need to select an area of the report that is not already occupied by data.

4 Go over to column AF, and click in row 1. Now, click the **arrow** under the clipboard image in the Clipboard pane, and select Transpose from the dropdown.

5 You should now have this selection of data displayed with the geographic region as the column header.

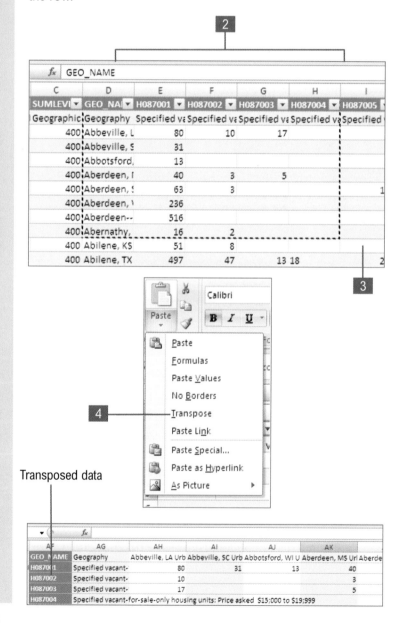

Transposed data

122

This next task should be familiar from Chapter 3. In fact, refreshing data in a spreadsheet report is essentially identical to running a background query in any other kind of report linked to your spreadsheet from external data.

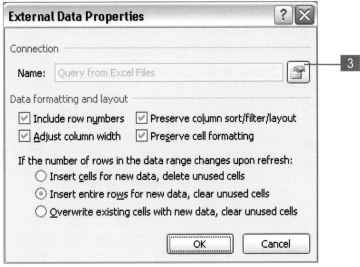

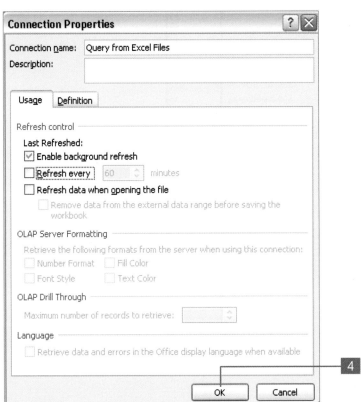

1 Make sure that you've selected a cell or cells within your spreadsheet report, and click the **Data** tab.

2 Click **Properties** to bring up the External Data Properties dialogue.

3 Click the **Connection Properties** button to the right of the Name field and ensure that the Enable background refresh box is checked.

4 Click **OK** to return to your spreadsheet report, where any updates from the source data will now be reflected in your report whenever data is refreshed.

?

Did you know?

Remember that you can also choose to refresh the data automatically at designated time intervals or whenever you open the file.

Using conditional formatting with reports

The crucial idea behind conditional formatting is that visual presentation can dramatically enhance your ability to convey the message your data is sending. Different types of visual presentation can also be used to convey different elements of your data. In this task, you'll learn where the conditional formatting tools are, what kinds of tools are available, and how to create your own custom formatting rules. The Conditional Formatting icon is located in the Styles group on the Home tab.

Click the **Conditional Formatting** icon, and you'll be presented with a list of formatting possibilities.

1 Highlight Cells Rules – This option lets you select cells based on how they respond to particular rules, such as whether they are greater than or less than a given value, for example. You can also highlight certain cells based on a rule that you create. We will look at this process shortly. In the image opposite, cells E3 through E28 have been selected, with a threshold value of 250. So, as you see, only values exceeding 250 are formatted.

2 Now, for the sake of the demonstration, click **Cancel** so you can check out the other formatting options available.

3 The Top/Bottom Rules will format the selected range in the same way as the Highlight Cells Rules, except this time, you'll be seeing the top or bottom 10 items, for example.

2

Greater Than	? ☒
Format cells that are GREATER THAN:	
250 with	Light Red Fill with Dark Red Text ▼
	OK Cancel

ID2 ▼	SUMLEVI ▼	GEO_NAI ▼	H087001 ▼	H087002 ▼	H087003 ▼	H087004 ▼
raphy l	Geographic	Geography	Specified v:	Specified v:	Specified v:	Specified v:
37	400	Abbeville, l	80	10	17	
64	400	Abbeville, S	31			
91	400	Abbotsford	13			
118	400	Aberdeen,	40	3	5	
145	400	Aberdeen,	63	3		
172	400	Aberdeen,	236			
199	400	Aberdeen--	516			
226	400	Abernathy,	16	2		
253	400	Abilene, KS	51	8		
280	400	Abilene, TX	497	47	13 18	
307	400	Abilene North (Robertson Unit), TX Urban Cluster				
334	400	Abingdon,	18		9	
361	400	Abingdon,	84			
388	400	Ada, OH Url	6			
415	400	Ada, OK Url	129	6	24 20	
442	400	Adairsville,	9			
469	400	Adel, GA Ur	41	4	2	
496	400	Adel, IA Url	7			
523	400	Adelanto, C	61			
550	400	Adjuntas, P	25		6	
577	400	Adrian, MI l	131		4	
631	400	Aguadilla--	1358	147	112 82	
658	400	Ahoskie, N(	21	3		
685	400	Airway Heig	27			
712	400	Ajo, AZ Urb	116	1	4 4	
739	400	Akron, NY l	21			
766	400	Akron, OH l	2394	53	17 17	

1

	A	B	C	D	E	F
1	GEO_ID	GEO_ID2	SUMLEVI	GEO_NAI	H087001	H087002
2	Geography	Geography	Geographic	Geography	Specified va	Specifie
3	40000US000	37	400	Abbeville, l	80	
4	40000US000	64	400	Abbeville, S	31	
5	40000US000	91	400	Abbotsford	13	
6	40000US001	118	400	Aberdeen,	40	
7	40000US001	145	400	Aberdeen,	63	
8	40000US001	172	400	Aberdeen,	236	
9	40000US001	199	400	Aberdeen--	516	
10	40000US002	226	400	Abernathy,	16	
11	40000US002	253	400	Abilene, KS	51	
12	40000US002	280	400	Abilene, TX	497	
13	40000US003	307	400	Abilene North (Robertson Unit),		
14	40000US003	334	400	Abingdon, l	18	
15	40000US003	361	400	Abingdon,	84	
16	40000US003	388	400	Ada, OH Url	6	
17	40000US004	415	400	Ada, OK Url	129	
18	40000US004	442	400	Adairsville,	9	
19	40000US004	469	400	Adel, GA Ur	41	
20	40000US004	496	400	Adel, IA Url	7	
21	40000US005	523	400	Adelanto, C	61	
22	40000US005	550	400	Adjuntas, P	25	
23	40000US005	577	400	Adrian, MI l	131	
24	40000US006	631	400	Aguadilla--	1358	
25	40000US006	658	400	Ahoskie, NC	21	
26	40000US006	685	400	Airway Heig	27	

5

4 The Data Bars create a graphic within each selected cell, giving you a very pointed visual comparison of your data. This option is very effective for drawing out certain cells with value that far exceeds the others in your range.

5 Notice how much clearer it is that the data in cell E24 largely exceeds the data in all other cells.

A	B	C	D	E	F	
GEO_ID	GEO_ID2	SUMLEVI	GEO_NAI	H087001	H087002	H08
Geography	Geography	Geographic	Geography	Specified va	Specified va	Spe
40000US000	37	400	Abbeville, l	80	10	
40000US000	64	400	Abbeville, S	31		
40000US000	91	400	Abbotsford	13		
40000US001	118	400	Aberdeen, l	40	3	
40000US001	145	400	Aberdeen,	63	3	
40000US001	172	400	Aberdeen,	236		
40000US001	199	400	Aberdeen--	516		
40000US002	226	400	Abernathy,	16	2	
40000US002	253	400	Abilene, KS	51	8	
40000US002	280	400	Abilene, TX	497	47	
40000US003	307	400	Abilene North (Robertson Unit), TX Urba			
40000US003	334	400	Abingdon, l	18		
40000US003	361	400	Abingdon,	84		
40000US003	388	400	Ada, OH Url	6		
40000US004	415	400	Ada, OK Url	129	6	
40000US004	442	400	Adairsville,	9		
40000US004	469	400	Adel, GA Ur	41	4	
40000US004	496	400	Adel, IA Url	7		
40000US005	523	400	Adelanto, C	61		
40000US005	550	400	Adjuntas, P	25		
40000US005	577	400	Adrian, MI l	131		
40000US006	631	400	Aguadilla--	1358	147	
40000US006	658	400	Ahoskie, NC	21	3	
40000US006	685	400	Airway Heig	27		
40000US007	712	400	Ajo, AZ Urb	116	1	
40000US007	739	400	Akron, NY l	21		
40000US007	766	400	Akron, OH l	2394	53	
40000US007	793	400	Alachua, FL	42		

6

7

6 The Color Scales option is one of my personal favourites. Because it represents your values as increasing or decreasing hues or colour values, a visually striking field of colour is produced. The effect is all the more pronounced the larger your selected data field is.

7 Again, the data in E24 really stands out, but it's also easier to discern which other values are relatively higher than the rest. You can also gain tighter control over exactly which data is presented by creating your own conditional formatting rules.

Using conditional formatting with reports (cont.)

8 Finally, you can choose from among Icon Sets, which are well suited to representing data that is being tracked in real time. For example, if you are linked to an external database, and you want values to be instantly identified if they surpass a certain amount, you may want to use Icon Sets to do this. An example of this would be to label values below a certain level with red traffic lights, values approaching a certain level with yellow, and values surpassing a certain level in red.

9 Using the default icon set rules, only cell E29 displays a green icon in our example. This is because Excel is tailored to business needs and when tracking sales, it's likely that you'd want your lowest sales to be the ones that are displayed as being 'in the red' as it were.

8

	A	B	C	D	E	F
	GEO_ID ▾	GEO_ID2 ▾	SUMLEVE ▾	GEO_NA ▾	H087001 ▾	H087002 ▾
	Geography	Geography	Geographic	Geography	Specified va	Specified v
	40000US000	37	400	Abbeville, l	80	1(
	40000US000	64	400	Abbeville, S	31	
	40000US000	91	400	Abbotsford	13	
	40000US001	118	400	Aberdeen,	40	
	40000US001	145	400	Aberdeen,	63	
	40000US001	172	400	Aberdeen,	236	
	40000US001	199	400	Aberdeen--	516	
	40000US002	226	400	Abernathy,	16	
	40000US002	253	400	Abilene, KS	51	
	40000US002	280	400	Abilene, TX	497	4
	40000US003	307	400	Abilene North (Robertson Unit), TX		
	40000US003	334	400	Abingdon, l	18	
	40000US003	361	400	Abingdon, V	84	
	40000US003	388	400	Ada, OH Urb	6	
	40000US004	415	400	Ada, OK Urb	129	
	40000US004	442	400	Adairsville,	9	
	40000US004	469	400	Adel, GA Ur	41	
	40000US004	496	400	Adel, IA Urb	7	
	40000US005	523	400	Adelanto, C	61	
	40000US005	550	400	Adjuntas, P	25	
	40000US005	577	400	Adrian, MI l	131	
	40000US006	631	400	Aguadilla--	1358	14
	40000US006	658	400	Ahoskie, N(	21	
	40000US006	685	400	Airway Heig	27	
	40000US007	712	400	Ajo, AZ Urba	116	
	40000US007	739	400	Akron, NY L	21	
	40000US007	766	400	Akron, OH L	2394	5
	40000US007	793	400	Alachua, FL	42	

9

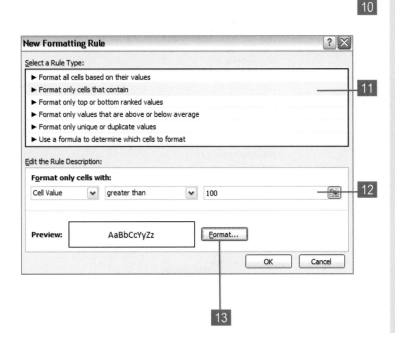

New Formatting Rule

Select a Rule Type:

- ▶ Format all cells based on their values
- ▶ Format only cells that contain
- ▶ Format only top or bottom ranked values
- ▶ Format only values that are above or below average
- ▶ Format only unique or duplicate values
- ▶ Use a formula to determine which cells to format

Edit the Rule Description:

Format all cells based on their values:

Format Style: 2-Color Scale

	Minimum	Maximum
Type:	Lowest Value	Highest Value
Value:	(Lowest value)	(Highest value)
Color:		

Preview:

OK   Cancel

New Formatting Rule

Select a Rule Type:

- ▶ Format all cells based on their values
- ▶ Format only cells that contain
- ▶ Format only top or bottom ranked values
- ▶ Format only values that are above or below average
- ▶ Format only unique or duplicate values
- ▶ Use a formula to determine which cells to format

Edit the Rule Description:

Format only cells with:

Cell Value | greater than | 100

Preview: AaBbCcYyZz | Format...

OK   Cancel

---

10 Click **New Formatting Rule** in the Styles group on the Home tab. You are presented with a range of possibilities, and within these possibilities, you can create practically any kind of rule imaginable. As you can see, you are given the option to format using formulas, format based on averages, format based on cell contents, etc.

11 Now, as your example, click on **Format only cells that contain**, which will give you first-hand experience of customised conditional formatting.

12 Select Cell Value in the left-hand field, greater than in the centre field, and 100 in the right-hand field. Now, only values that are greater than 100 will be formatted in your range.

13 Click **Format**, and you'll be taken to the Format Cells dialogue, where you can select any colour you wish.

Using conditional formatting with reports (cont.)

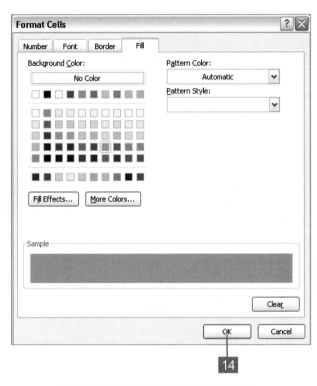

14 In the example, I've used an olive green hue. Click **OK** to exit, and **OK** again when you arrive at the first dialogue. Now, all values within your range containing a number higher than 100 should be formatted with whatever colour you selected.

You may not find exactly what you're looking for from among the proposed default rules. Not to worry, because Excel 2007 provides the ability to create your own custom rule that can be applied to your spreadsheet. You access this tool by selecting New Rule from the bottom of the list in the Styles group, or go to Manage Rules, where you can delete or modify pre-existing rules in addition to being able to add a new rule.

400 Abbeville, L	80	10
400 Abbeville, S	31	
400 Abbotsford,	13	
400 Aberdeen, I	40	3
400 Aberdeen, S	63	3
400 Aberdeen, V	236	
400 Aberdeen--	516	
400 Abernathy,	16	2
400 Abilene, KS	51	8
400 Abilene, TX	497	47
400 Abilene North (Robertson Unit), TX U		
400 Abingdon, I	18	
400 Abingdon, V	84	
400 Ada, OH Urb	6	
400 Ada, OK Urb	129	6
400 Adairsville,	9	
400 Adel, GA Ur	41	4
400 Adel, IA Urb	7	
400 Adelanto, C	61	
400 Adjuntas, PI	25	
400 Adrian, MI U	131	
400 Aguadilla--I	1358	147
400 Ahoskie, NC	21	3
400 Airway Heig	27	
400 Ajo, AZ Urba	116	1
400 Akron, NY U	21	
400 Akron, OH U	2394	53

Business intelligence is an industry term in the field of data management that's become relatively standard jargon over the past 10 or so years. When people refer to business intelligence in reference to working with data, they mean, specifically, analysing data in a way that enables better business decision making. Here's a hypothetical example to better illustrate what's meant by business intelligence. Let's say that you were only interested in housing that was between $50,000 and $100,000, and you only wanted to look at regions with at least 500 housing units for sale. In the previous example, you saw how conditional formatting could be used to highlight certain data. Well, if you're using conditional formatting in a way that optimises your decision-making abilities as you speculate on real estate investment, then you're already using business intelligence techniques. Using charts has never been easier than it is in Excel 2007, making their application to business intelligence equally accessible.

Using charts to find business intelligence

1 First, go to the Insert tab. This is where you'll find the available charts. You can choose from Column, Line, Pie, Bar, Area or Scatter charts. When you click the image for each category, you will see more specific types of charts in this category appear.

The final group contains more specialised charts such as Doughnut Charts, Bubble Charts, Radar Charts, etc. Some of these are best tailored to particular kinds of data; the Stock Charts, for example, will only work to represent actual stock prices.

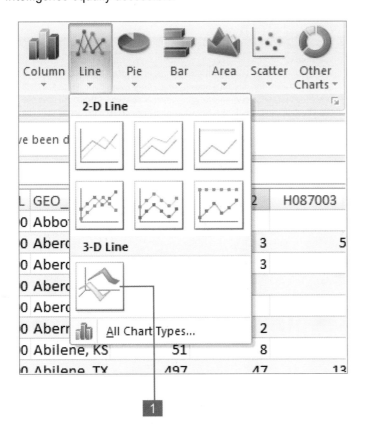

Using charts to find business intelligence (cont.)

2 The data you're working with here is effectively expressed by a 3-D Column Chart. This is because you have a lot of data, and it represents a snapshot of a particular situation. To keep things simple, and create a chart that's easy to see and understand, select the housing price data for only the first four geographic areas in your table. Start by selecting cells D1 through D6, and then drag your selection all the way to the edge of the report, at column AC. Click the **copy** icon in the Clipboard group on the Home tab (or just hit [Ctrl]+[C]).

3 Now, you'll put your newly acquired column-arranging skills to use by clicking cell **AJ**, and then clicking the **arrow** under the Paste icon in the Clipboard group and choosing Transpose from the drop-down menu.

Once your chart is produced, you'll see that having geographic regions as columns makes a lot of sense in this scenario.

Geography	Abbeville, L	Abbeville, S	Abbotsford,	Aberdeen, MS Urban Cluster
Specified va	80	31	13	40
Specified va	10			3
Specified va	17			5
Specified vacant-for-sale-only housing units: Price asked $15;000 to $19;999				
Specified va	5			3
Specified vacant-for-sale-only housing units: Pri				2
Specified va	6	5		14
Specified va	1			
Specified va	5		1	7
Specified va	10	6		
Specified va	3	15	7	
Specified vacant-for-sale-only housi			1	3
Specified va	2	5		
Specified va	1		4	3
Specified va	14			
Specified va	3			
Specified va	3			
Specified vacant-for-sale-only housing units: Price asked $175;000 to $199;999				
Specified vacant-for-sale-only housing units: Price asked $200;000 to $249;999				
Specified vacant-for-sale-only housing units: Price asked $250;000 to $299;999				
Specified vacant-for-sale-only housing units: Price asked $300;000 to $399;999				
Specified vacant-for-sale-only housing units: Price asked $400;000 to $499;999				
Specified vacant-for-sale-only housing units: Price asked $500;000 to $749;999				
Specified vacant-for-sale-only housing units: Price asked $750;000 to $999;999				
Specified vacant-for-sale-only housing units: Price asked $1;000;000 or more				

2

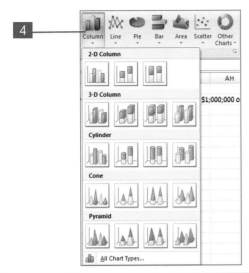

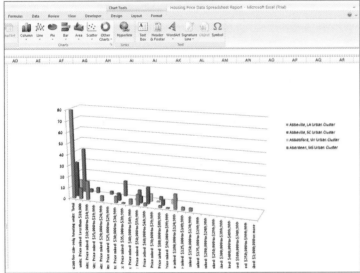

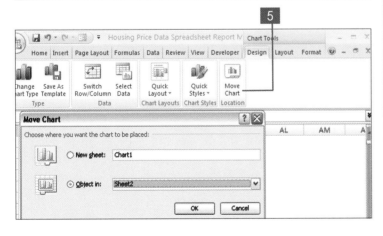

7

4 Select and copy the new table you've produced, and then click on the **Column** icon in the Charts group on the Insert tab, and select the 3-D Column option that's further to the right on that row.

You'll have to do a little bit of dragging and dropping to get all of the images in your chart to appear in a clear and legible way. But when you're done, it should look something like the adjacent image.

5 Note that when you select inside the chart, a new set of tools, called the Chart Tools, will appear in the ribbon. Click on the **Design**, **Layout**, and **Format** tabs to briefly see what kind of tools are available on each. Now, because this sheet is getting a little cluttered, click on the **Design** tab, and choose Move Chart in the Location group.

You're going to move the chart to Sheet 2 so you can have more room to work freely with it. It will appear in the same place it was at in the original sheet, so drag it over to A1.

Using charts to find business intelligence (cont.)

One important aspect of business intelligence is that it accesses, analyses and presents data in such a way that you don't have to concentrate on what it is you're looking at, but rather, on the decision-making process informed by your data.

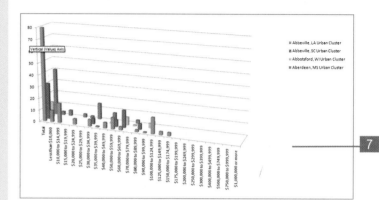

6 You'll notice that the labels on the x-axis are a bit long-winded; there are more concise ways of presenting this information. Remember that this chart is a visualisation of the table in your first sheet. The simplest way to alter this data is to go back to Sheet1, and delete the text 'Specified vacant-for-sale-only housing units: Price asked' from your table. Don't worry, that text will remain in the original report table from which you copied the data.

7 There's one more minor issue: for some reason, the numbers linked to the original data were produced with a semicolon instead of a comma separating their hundreds from their thousands place. Select all the cells containing numbers and do a Find and Replace, substituting the symbol ';' with ','. Go back to Sheet 2, and your chart should now look as the image.

A few more tweaks, and you'll have a nice-looking chart that you could present at a board meeting, for example.

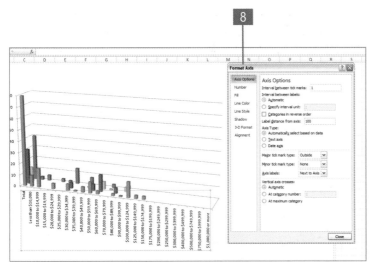

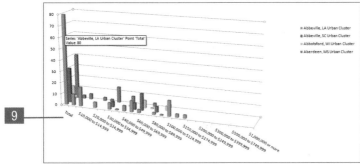

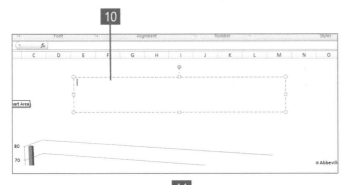

Using charts to find business intelligence (cont.)

8 The x-axis labels might be a bit more aesthetically pleasing, and fit in the space provided more effectively if they were at an angle. Most of the modifications that you'll do can be accomplished with the Chart Tools, as in this particular instance, where you'll use the Layout tab. Start by selecting the x-axis labels, or the Horizontal (Category) Axis. Click the **Format Selection** option in the Current Selection group on the Layout tab to open the Format Axis dialogue.

9 Next, click **Alignment**, and, in Custom angle field, type 30. Your values will immediately be presented at a 30 degree angle. Now click **Close**.

10 Finally, because you removed some of the information from the labels on the x-axis, you'll add a text box to ensure that anyone looking at your chart will know exactly what information it contains. Click on **Text Box** in the Insert group, on the Layout tab.

11 Right-click the text and change the font size to 20.

Tables and charts in reports 133

Using charts to find business intelligence (cont.)

12 Now, click on the **Format** tab, in the Shape Styles group, and select a border. The example uses a purple border. Last of all, select your preferred Word Art Style, also from the Format tab.

Now you have a clean, easily discernible chart that's laid out in a way that takes the guesswork out of looking at data when you're trying to make more important, higher-level business decisions.

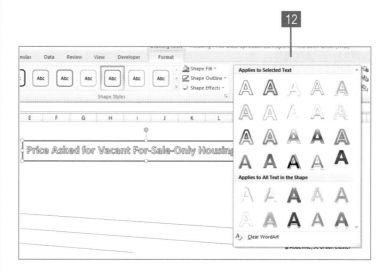

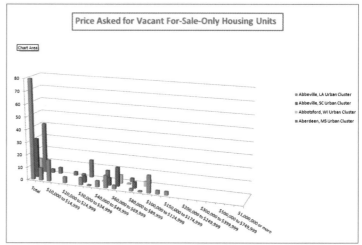

You've already got a great-looking chart, but why stop there? Excel 2007 makes it easier than ever before to make your chart really shine. The interface for applying pattern fills has been replaced by the Shape Styles group, which lets you easily add graphics and professional-quality graphical elements to your chart. Everything you'll need can once again be found in the Chart Tools.

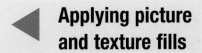

Applying picture and texture fills

1 Click anywhere in your chart to bring up the Chart Tools, go to the Shape Styles group, and click **Shape Fill**.

2 Choose Picture from the drop-down list, and you'll be able to browse your hard drive to find whatever picture you'd like to add. In the example, you'll just add one of the sample pictures provided by Microsoft. But, of course, you can choose whatever picture you want. Click **Insert**, and now your chart has a nice background image.

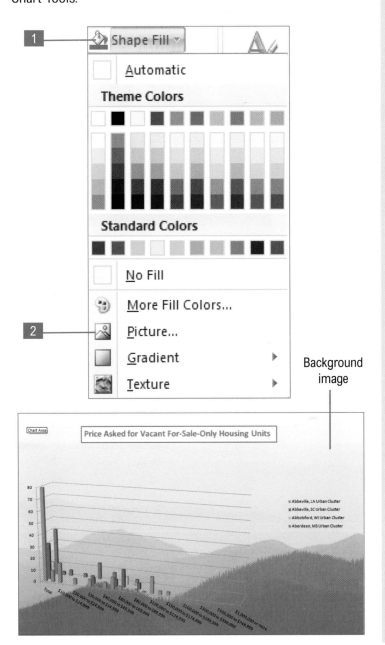

Background image

Applying picture and texture fills (cont.)

3 Adding a texture fill involves a similar procedure. Click inside the text box where you added the title of your chart, and then click once again on **Shape Fill**. This time, however, select Texture, and you'll be presented with a series of textures to choose from.

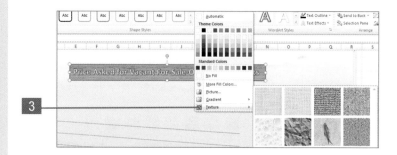

4 Select Oak, which goes well with the mountain theme of the sample background image. Your title will now have an aesthetically pleasing background texture.

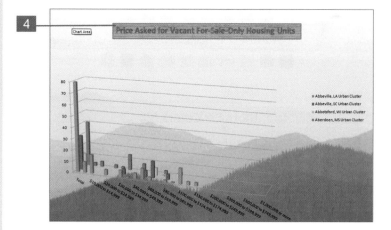

Excel 2007 also gives you the ability to combine different types of charts on the same axes, which can be very helpful when comparing different kinds of data. In the example of the chart you've created, you might want to change the chart type for one geographic area so as to throw it into relief in relation to the others.

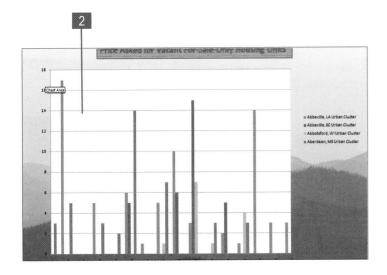

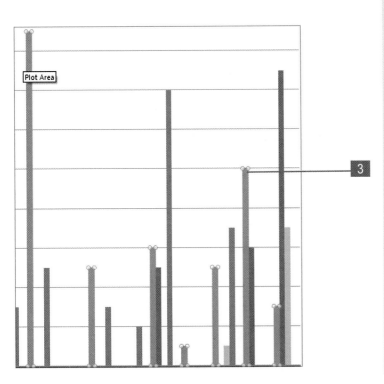

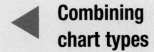
1 First, because combining chart types works best in a 2-D arena, and there are a few more categories than the data actually requires, go back to the first sheet, and delete all rows for values above $174,000 because there is no data to fill them. Also, for the sake of a consistent layout, delete the Total column.

2 Now, return to Sheet2, click **Change Chart Type** from the ribbon, and choose Clustered Column. Your chart should now look as the image.

3 The object of this task is to differentiate the visual presentation for Abbeville, LA, from the rest of your geographic regions. So click on the bars representing Abbeville, LA, within the chart. Make sure that bubbles appear on all of the bars, or the reformatting won't work.

Tables and charts in reports 137

Combining chart types (cont.)

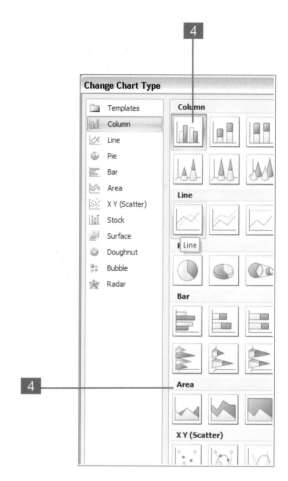

4 Now click **Change Chart Type**, and choose Area. The data for Abbeville, LA, will be presented as an area graph on the same axes as the columns representing your other data.

Combining column and line charts is especially helpful when comparing data that changes over time with data that does not.

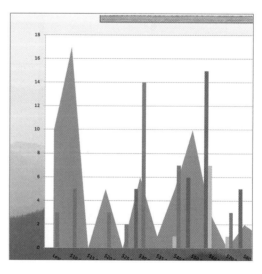

Another great thing about Excel 2007 is that all of the new tools available for modifying charts are also available for PivotCharts. In fact, the PivotChart Tools that appear when you create a PivotChart differ from the regular Chart Tools only in that they also include an Analyze tab. Of course, when you create a PivotChart, you have all flexibility that it provides.

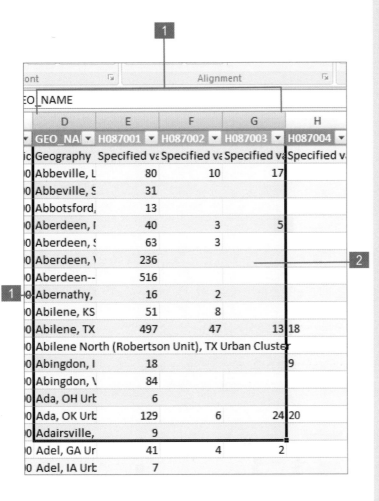

1 You want a good amount of data to create your sample PivotChart, but not so much that it's hard to create a coherent image. Go to Sheet1, and select cells from columns D to G, and from rows 1 to 18.

2 Make sure that you've selected only the aforementioned cells to be represented in your PivotChart by clicking in the provided range field.

	GEO_NA	H087001	H087002	H087003	H087004
ic	Geography	Specified va	Specified va	Specified va	Specified v.
0	Abbeville, L	80	10	17	
0	Abbeville, S	31			
0	Abbotsford,	13			
0	Aberdeen, I	40	3	5	
0	Aberdeen, S	63	3		
0	Aberdeen, \	236			
0	Aberdeen--	516			
0	Abernathy,	16	2		
0	Abilene, KS	51	8		
0	Abilene, TX	497	47	13	18
0	Abilene North (Robertson Unit), TX Urban Cluster				
0	Abingdon, I	18			9
0	Abingdon, \	84			
0	Ada, OH Urb	6			
0	Ada, OK Urb	129	6	24	20
0	Adairsville,	9			
0	Adel, GA Ur	41	4	2	
0	Adel, IA Urb	7			

7

Modifying PivotCharts (cont.)

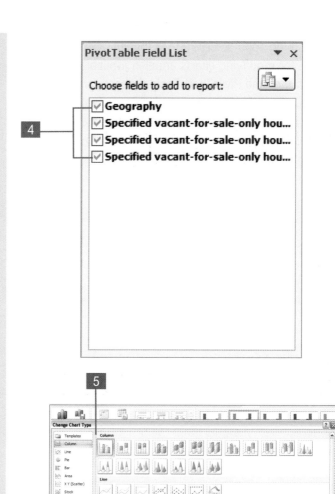

3. Select PivotChart from the Tables group in the Insert tab, and choose New Worksheet.

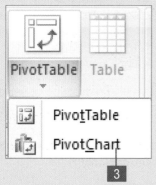

4. Check all four boxes in the PivotTable Field List, and arrange the fields as shown in the image.

5. Now, just as you did with regular charts, go to the Change Chart Type on the Design tab. Choose Stacked Column in 3-D and click **OK**.

6. Now you can take advantage of all the same customisation options you had with regular charts, but with the added flexibility of a PivotChart.

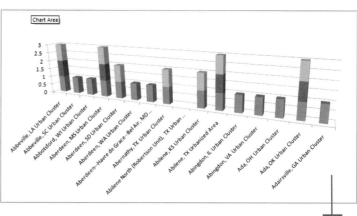

Securing your Excel data

Introduction

Security is a major concern when working with financial records or other data in Excel. You need to be able to manage which content is displayed and which is blocked. You also need to protect your data by locking it so unauthorised users cannot alter it. And you need to protect yourself from viruses and other harmful software that infect macros. In previous versions of Excel, security was managed by means of prompts to the user. In Excel 2007, security has been automated to some extent. In addition, features like encryption and digital signatures have been integrated into the program in a streamlined way. This chapter describes some simple tasks you can do to make working with data in Excel safe, and to control how the program manages security.

What you'll do

Protect a workbook with passwords

Lock elements within a workbook

Change workbook protection

Adjust macro security settings

Recover lost or forgotten Excel 2007 passwords

Test Excel's macro protection

Protect a workbook with a digital signature

Create your own Digital ID

View a digital signature

Encrypt an Excel workbook

Security concerns and Microsoft Excel

In an effort to raise data security to a new level, Excel, like other Office 2007 files, handles security differently from previous versions. It makes use of a component called the Trust Center, which acts as a central repository for all of your Office 2007 security settings. In previous versions of Excel, you were prompted to respond to security warnings when opening a workbook. Now, all content that Excel considers potentially dangerous is blocked without any warnings displayed. If content is blocked, you are notified by means of the Trust Bar, which appears at the top of the application window. You can then click the bar to unblock the content.

You'll find the Trust Center in the **Office** Center:

1. Click the **Office** button.

2. Click **Excel Options**.

3. Click the **Trust Center** option on the left side of the Options window.

4. Click **Trust Center Settings**...

5. Click on one of the categories on the left side to view Trust Center settings and change them if you wish.

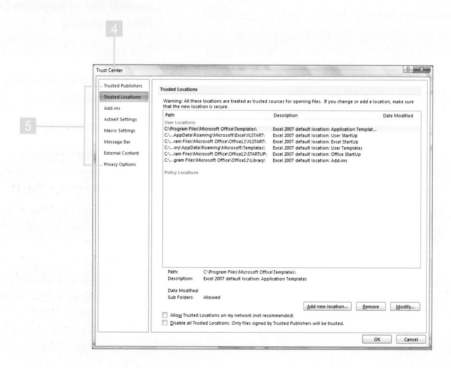

Excel 2007 enables you to protect an entire workbook by means of advanced encryption. You protect an entire workbook by assigning two separate passwords. One password is encrypted; it prevents unauthorised users from opening and viewing the workbook. This is the highest level of security you can create to protect a workbook. The second password is not encrypted; it allows users to open the file and modify it as well as save changes. You don't have to use both passwords with any particular workbook. You should, however, always protect a file by assigning the unencrypted password that allows users to modify data. The second encrypted password can be added to protect especially sensitive files.

1 Click the **Office** button.

2 Choose Save As.

Did you know?

The same password restrictions apply to Word 2007 files, PowerPoint® 2007 presentations, and other Office 2007 files. If you lose a password, Excel cannot recover it for you. You can download and install a special application designed to recover passwords, however; see 'Recovering lost or forgotten Excel 2007 passwords' for more.

Protecting a workbook with passwords (cont.)

3 Click the **down arrow** next to Tools.

4 Choose General Options.

5 Type an encrypted password that users will need simply to open the file.

6 Type an unencrypted password that users will need to modify and save the file.

7 Optionally, check the box to give users the choice of opening a read-only version of the file. Users can then use the read-only version or a modifiable version, depending on their choice.

8 Click **OK**.

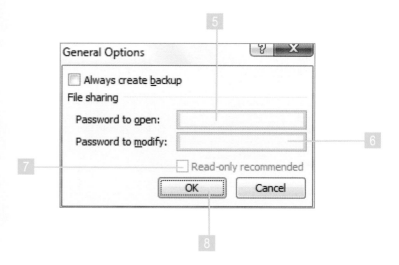

For your information

Even if you assign one or more passwords to a workbook, your security can be undone if you use a simple, insecure password that can be easily guessed, such as 'administrator' or 'password'. Make sure your password does not contain recognisable words in the dictionary, but mixes upper- and lowercase characters as well as letters and numerals. For instance, the password Gs2008tQ is strong, while Queen2008 is weak.

Sometimes, you want others in your organisation to be able to view or edit workbooks, while protecting data in parts of the current worksheet. You might have some dates and figures that must remain constant, for instance. If that's the case, you can use the Protect Sheet control to establish element-level protection for the worksheet.

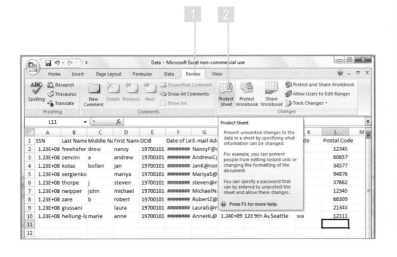

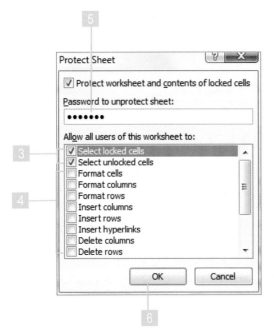

Locking elements within a workbook

1 Click **Review**.

2 Click **Protect Sheet**.

3 Check the boxes next to any elements in the worksheet that you want to protect.

4 Uncheck the boxes next to any elements in the worksheet that you want to be able to edit.

5 Enter a password to prevent users from undoing your protection.

6 Click **OK**.

For your information

The Password to unprotect sheet box is useful because it prevents individuals from being able to unprotect any elements you have protected. If you don't enter a password, anyone can click **Review**, click **Protect Sheet**, and uncheck an element so they can edit it. If you do enter a password, if someone attempts to make changes to the protection of any element, they are prompted to enter a password first.

Changing workbook protection

You can adjust or add levels of password security for a worksheet or workbook from Excel's Review tab. If you have already assigned password protection to a workbook, the Protect Sheet button lets you assign a password that users can enter to *unprotect* the worksheet. The Protect Workbook button lets you assign a password that protects the workbook's structure or individual windows.

Assigning an unprotect password

1 Click **Review**.

2 Click **Protect Sheet**.

3 Type a password in the box labelled Password to unprotect sheet.

4 Click **OK**.

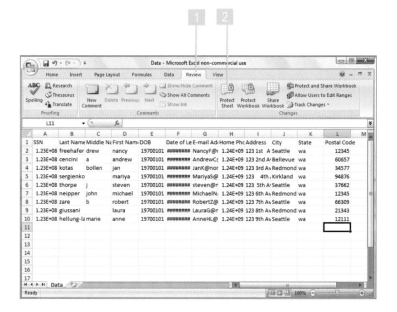

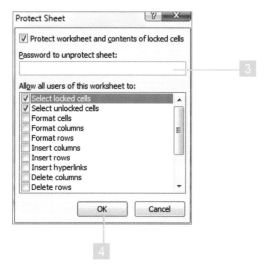

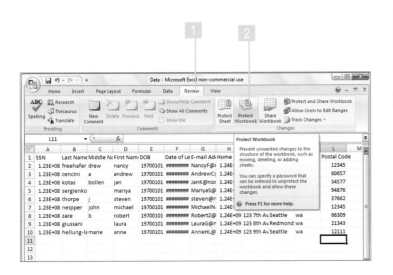

Fine-tune workbook protection

1 Click **Review**.

2 Click **Protect Workbook**.

3 Check this box to protect the workbook's structure. This keeps users from viewing hidden worksheets, renaming worksheets or adding new worksheets.

4 Check this box to protect the current window. This prevents users from changing the size and position of a workbook's windows when it is opened, or from moving or closing windows.

5 Type a password to enable users to make changes to either the structure or the window.

6 Click **OK**.

Adjusting macro security settings

Macros are convenient; they are sets of commands or steps that you set up and run automatically. Macros have a bad reputation because they can cause virus infections, but the truth is that as long as you have antivirus software running and you take advantage of Office 2007's security features, you should be protected. You can download macros that others have created to help you save time. But make sure you have your trust levels adjusted so you download only macros from reliable sources.

1 Click the **Office** button.

2 Click **Excel Options**.

3 Click **Trust Center**.

4 Click **Trust Center Settings**.

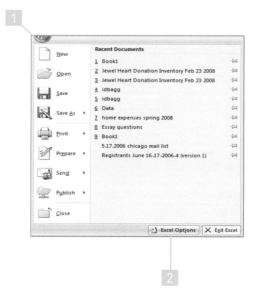

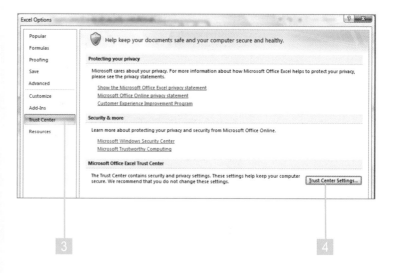

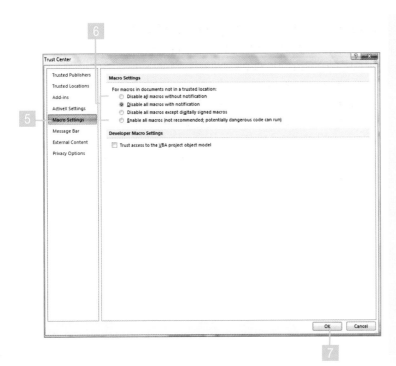

5 Click **Macro Settings**.

6 Choose one of the four options that determine how Excel handles macros.

7 Click **OK**.

Table 7.1 Excel Macro Settings

Setting	What it does
Disable all macros without notification	Blocks all macros; choose this only if you don't want to use any macros
Disable all macros with notification	Macros won't work, but if one is present, you see a security alert so you can choose to run it if you wish
Disable all macros except digitally signed macros	If a macro has been 'signed' by a trusted publisher with an encrypted file called a digital signature, Excel runs it automatically
Enable all macros	Excel runs all macros automatically without notifying you and without security protection

Recovering lost or forgotten Excel 2007 passwords

It's important to create complex passwords that are difficult to crack in order to protect your Excel data. However, if you lose or forget one of those passwords, Excel doesn't include a way to recover a password – unless you use the same brute-force password techniques you are trying to avoid. You can, however, download a password recovery program called Excel 2007 Password Recovery by LastBit Software (**http://www.lastbit.com**); if the application finds a lost password, you are asked to pay a service fee, after which the password is sent to you.

1 Download the Excel 2007 Password Recovery program.

2 Double-click the downloaded application to install it.

3 When a User Account Control dialogue box appears, click **Continue**.

4 Go through the setup routine.

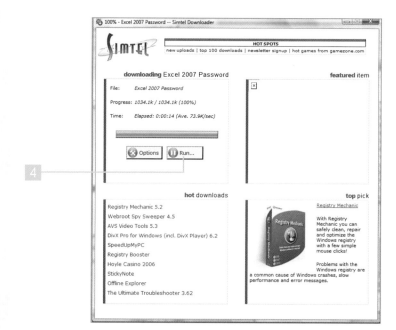

5 When the program window opens, click **Start**.

6 Scroll down to the bottom of the next screen and click the words **Click here**.

8

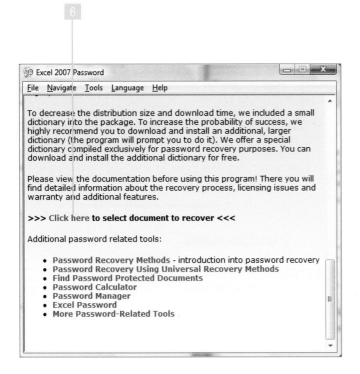

To decrease the distribution size and download time, we included a small dictionary into the package. To increase the probability of success, we highly recommend you to download and install an additional, larger dictionary (the program will prompt you to do it). We offer a special dictionary compiled exclusively for password recovery purposes. You can download and install the additional dictionary for free.

Please view the documentation before using this program! There you will find detailed information about the recovery process, licensing issues and warranty and additional features.

>>> Click here to select document to recover <<<

Additional password related tools:

- Password Recovery Methods - introduction into password recovery
- Password Recovery Using Universal Recovery Methods
- Find Password Protected Documents
- Password Calculator
- Password Manager
- Excel Password
- More Password-Related Tools

Recovering lost or forgotten Excel 2007 passwords (cont.)

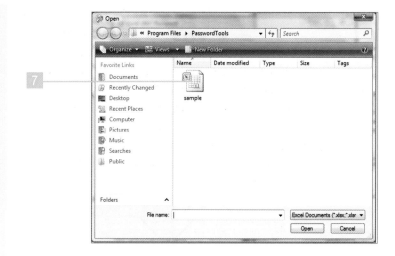

7 Locate the file you want to open and double-click it, or double-click the Sample file to try the program out.

8 Select a recovery method.

9 Click **Next**.

10 Wait while the program 'cracks' your password. If the process takes too long, choose a faster method.

11 Click **Cancel** to abort the detection process.

12 Follow the steps on subsequent screens to recover your password.

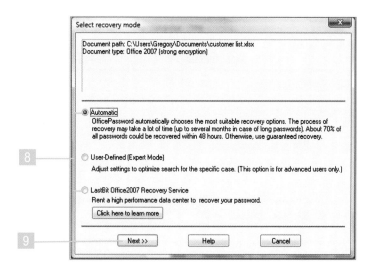

For your information

The Excel 2007 Password Recovery application works only with passwords that prevent unauthorised users from opening a file, not passwords that allow file modification.

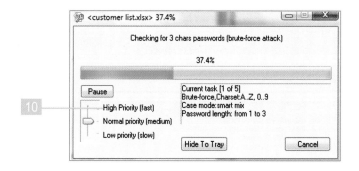

Setting macro protection levels is only one step of the security process. The second part is learning to use the notification tools that are built into the application. To test out macro protection, download and then open an evaluation copy of a document that uses a macro, such as the Investment and Business Valuation template found at **http://www.business-spreadsheets.com/investval.htm**. Then follow the steps described here, which show not only Excel's macro protection but the various levels of protection Windows Vista provides for downloading a file from the internet.

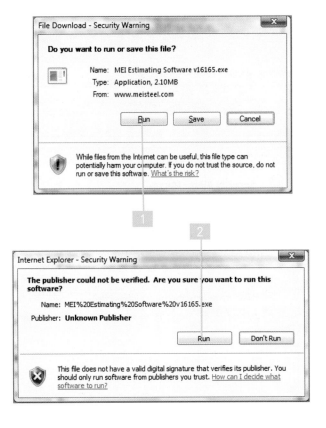

1. When the File Download – Security Warning screen appears, click **Run**.

2. If a second security warning screen appears, click **Run** again.

3. When a User Account Control screen appears, click **Allow**.

8

Testing Excel's macro protection (cont.)

4. When the file downloads, double-click it to open it in Excel.

5. Click **Options** in the security bar.

6. Click **Enable this content**.

7. Click **OK**.

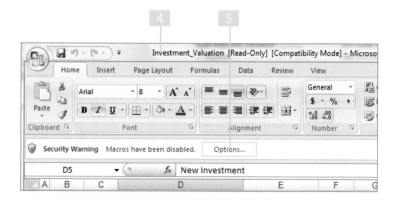

One of the criteria for accepting a macro is the fact that it has been protected by a digital signature. A digital signature, also known as a Digital ID, certifies that the person who claims to be the originator of the software or the file is its legitimate owner. You can obtain your own Digital ID and attach it to a workbook to protect it.

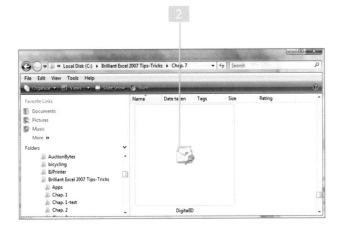

Protecting a workbook with a digital signature

If you don't want to create your own Digital ID, you can go to a site such as the Iridium Digital ID Service (**http://iridium.is-a-geek.com/DigitalID**) and obtain your own Digital ID. Or you can download an ID from one of Microsoft's approved certificate services as described below.

When the Digital ID is sent as an attachment to the email address you supplied, save the attachment to your file system.

Click the **Office** button.

Point to Prepare.

Choose Add a Digital Signature.

Protecting a workbook with a digital signature (cont.)

6 Click here if you haven't obtained a Digital ID/Signature yet.

7 Choose one of the Microsoft certificate providers and follow the steps shown online to obtain a Digital ID.

Did you know?

You can also add a digital signature to a file as part of a visible signature line. You create a signature line and then add the signature to it, much as you would sign a letter or other form. Visible signatures are primarily used with Word files, though they can be added to Excel workbooks as well.

Excel 2007 includes the ability to generate a digital signature for you. As you'll see, this signature is more than just you saying who you are. The signature, like others you can obtain online, includes a private key: a complex encoded block of characters generated by an algorithm. Follow steps 1 through 7 in the preceding task. Then follow these steps.

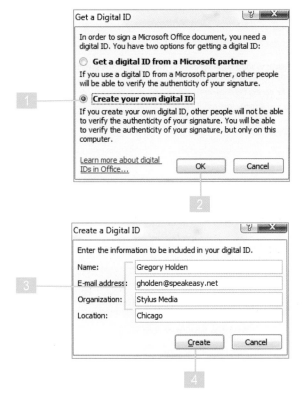

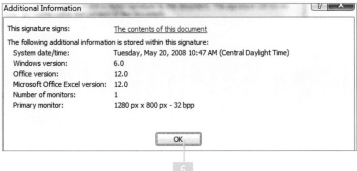

Creating your own Digital ID

1 Click **Create your own digital ID**.

2 Click **OK**.

3 Fill in the information about yourself that you want to include with your signature.

4 Click **Create**.

5 Click **OK**.

8

Creating your
own digital ID
(cont.)

6 Optionally, type a reason or explanation for adding a signature.

7 Click **Sign**.

8 Click **OK**.

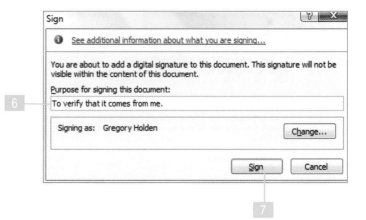

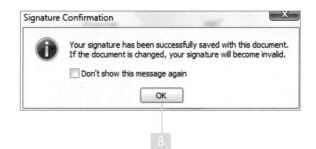

Whether you create a signature or you open a workbook that includes someone else's signature, it's a good idea to take a look at the digital file and understand what you are looking at. That way, you can be sure the signature is genuine and the workbook is reliable.

Viewing a digital signature

Look for the red ribbon icon in the status bar that indicates a file has been digitally signed and single-click the icon.

Pass your mouse over the signer's name and click the down arrow.

Click Signature Details.

Notice whether the signature is considered valid or not.

Click **View**.

8

Viewing a digital signature (cont.)

⑥ Click **Details** to view when the signature was created as well as the algorithm used to create it.

⑦ When you're done, click **OK**.

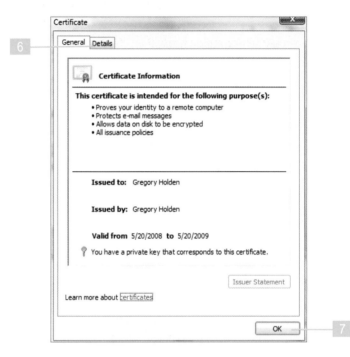

If one of your Excel documents contains sensitive data that you don't want co-workers or family members to access, you can encrypt it. This provides another layer of protection over and above using a password to open or modify a file. In the process of encrypting a file, you assign a password to it. The downside of assigning another password to encrypt the file is the need to remember it. On the other hand, if you want to provide the highest level of protection possible, you can add encryption as well as the other protection layers described earlier.

Encrypting an Excel workbook

1   Click the **Office** button.

2   Point to Prepare.

3   Choose Encrypt Document.

Encrypting an Excel workbook (cont.)

4 Type a password that is easy to remember, yet secure.

5 Click **OK**.

6 Re-enter the password when prompted to do so.

7 Click **OK**.

8 When you or someone else attempts to reopen the file after closing it, type the password.

9 Click **OK**.

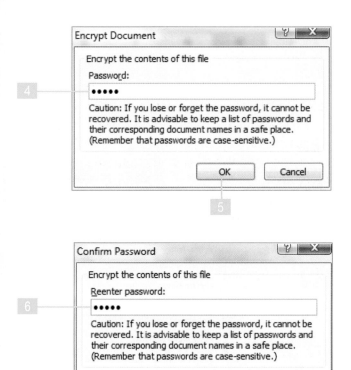

Excel and the internet

Introduction

Excel 2007 gives you a variety of ways to retrieve data from the web. You don't have to open a web page to make a connection, either. You can either cut and paste data from a web page, or make a live data connection through a web query. And you have options for making web queries, too: you can select the data yourself by working in 'Classic Mode' or use a shortcut called Select Similar, which is available in the Advanced Mode version of New Web Query. The important thing is that you can make live data connections to websites and live hyperlinks to web pages or other spreadsheets, and refresh the data with just a couple of mouse clicks.

Creating a simple web query by copying and pasting

One way to obtain data you see on a web page is simply to copy it in your web browser and paste it into Excel. The nice thing about this method is that it's simple – it's something you can do on the spur of the moment, as you are viewing a web page – and the data can be updated by refreshing your spreadsheet. If the data on the web has changed since your last refresh, the updated data will be displayed in Excel. You don't have to recopy the information to update it, in other words.

1 Open the web page that contains the data you want to copy and scroll across it to select it.

2 Press [Ctrl]+[C] to copy the data to your computer clipboard.

3 Make Excel the active application, and click the cell where you want to paste the data.

4 Click the **Home** tab.

5 Click **Paste**. Be sure to click the Paste button itself and not the drop-down arrow beneath it.

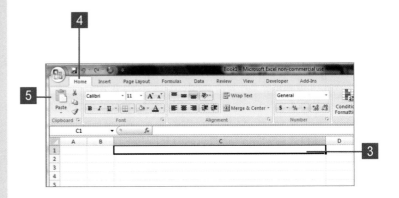

6 Mouse over the Paste Options button in the bottom right-hand corner of the data, click the **down arrow**, and choose Create Refreshable Web Query.

The New Web Query dialogue box opens. You might have to wait a minute or so for the data to be retrieved from the remote website.

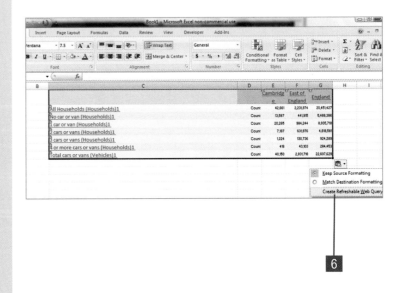

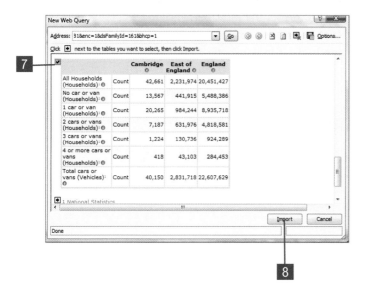

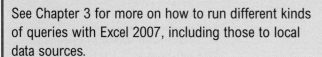

7 When the page appears in New Web Query, scroll down to find the data you want. Click the **arrow buttons** to select the refreshable data.

8 Click **Import**.

See also

See Chapter 3 for more on how to run different kinds of queries with Excel 2007, including those to local data sources.

9

Querying a web page and importing full formatting

Sometimes, data isn't all you want to import from web pages. You might want to import hyperlinks and other formatting that is specific to HyperText Markup Languages (HTML), one of the sets of instructions used to format content on the web. But there are potential problems with this method as well. In this task you'll see what happens when you import HTML formatting as well as data. You may not want to spend the time needed to reformat the information, but it's at least good to know that this option exists if it's important to import a web page and make it look exactly as it does online.

1 Open a new worksheet and click cell **A1**.

2 Click the **Data** tab.

3 Click **From Web** in the Get External Data tool group.

4 When the Web Query dialogue box appears, click **Options**.

5 Click **Full HTML Formatting**.

6 Click **OK**.

The Web Query Options dialogue box closes and you return to the Web Query dialogue box.

7 Type the address of a web page that contains data you can download. For instance, you could type an example on the National Health Services Scotland site, such as:
http://www.neighbourhood. statistics.gov.uk/dissemination/LeadTableView.do?a=3& b=276891&c=Cambridge&d= 13&e=16&g=425971&i=1001 x1003x1004&m=0&r=1&s=1 214313797880&enc=1&dsFa milyId=91

8 Click **Go** (or press [Enter]).

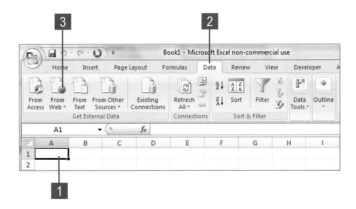

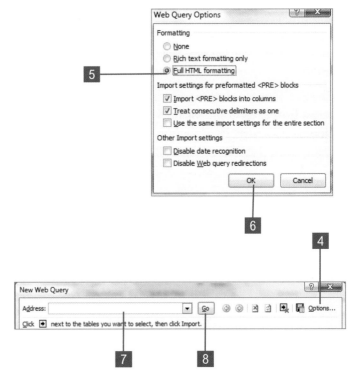

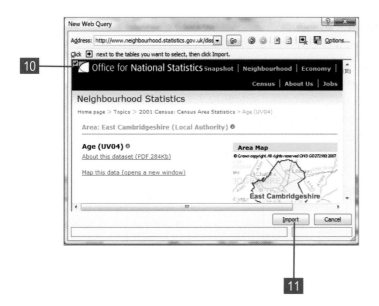

9 If a File Download box appears asking if you want to Open or Save the file, click **Open**.

10 When the web page opens in the New Web Query dialogue box, click the **arrow** in the upper left corner to select the entire page.

11 Click **Import**.

12 Click **OK**.

13 When the web page is imported, scroll down and inspect it. You'll probably see that, first, you have imported much more content than you actually need. Second, much of the formatting probably wasn't translated correctly in the importing process, so you'll need to reformat it using the familiar formatting controls on the Home tab.

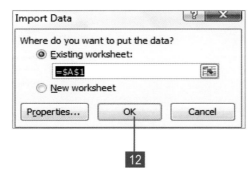

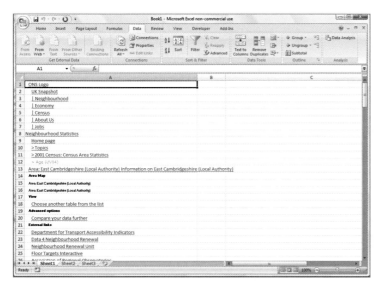

Making and saving a basic web query

Most of the time, when you're making a query to a remote web page, you don't necessarily want to import all the HTML formatting that goes with the page. Rather, you just want the information. You do that by following the steps shown in the previous section but without clicking the Full HTML Formatting option. Once you make a query, you can save it so you can run it again any time.

Making the query

1 Follow steps 1–3 in the preceding task.

2 Type the address of the web page to which you want to connect.

3 Click **Go** (or press [Enter]).

4 If a File Download box appears asking if you want to Open or Save the file, click **Open**.

5 Click the **yellow arrow** in the upper left corner to select the entire page.

6 Click **Import**.

7 Decide whether you want the data to open in a new or existing worksheet.

8 Click **OK**.

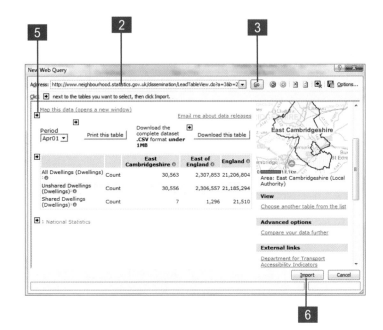

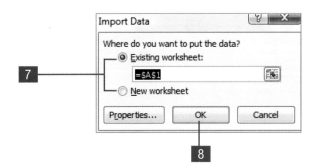

Making and saving a basic web query (cont.)

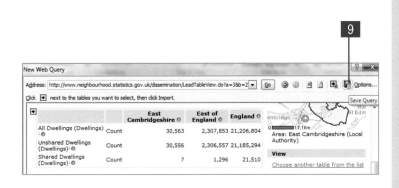

Saving the query

9 Click the **Save Query** button in the New Web Query dialogue box.

10 When the Save Query dialogue box opens, select a location on your file system where you want to save the query.

11 Type a name for the query.

12 Click **Save**.

13 Click **Cancel**.

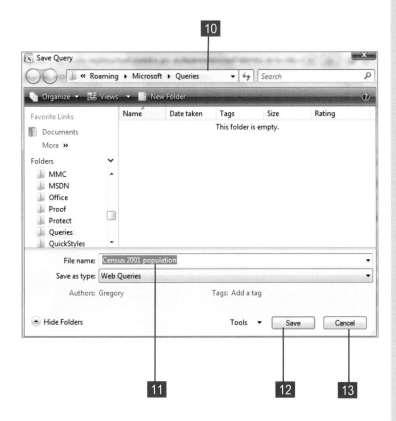

? 9

Did you know?

By default, queries are saved in a Queries folder that was created when Microsoft Excel was stored, and which makes them easier for Excel to find. You don't necessarily need to save queries in the same folder as the worksheet that contains the data from the query.

Retrieving a
saved web query

▶

Once you save a query, it's easy to call it up if you want to reconnect to the web page from which you need to retrieve data. Queries are saved with the .iqy filename extension so they can be imported quickly into other files. This is a great timesaving tip because it prevents you from having to perform the same queries over and over in different workbooks.

1 Click the **Data** tab.

2 Click **Existing Connections**.

3 If you don't see the saved query, choose a location from which to look for it.

4 Click the web query you want to perform.

5 Click **Open**.

6 Choose whether you want the data to open in an existing or new worksheet.

7 Click **OK**.

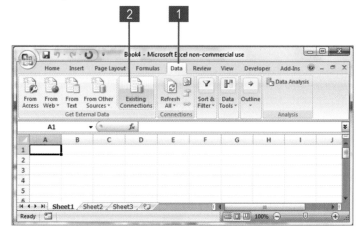

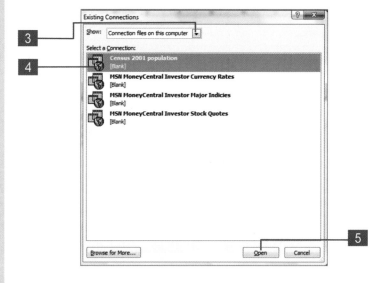

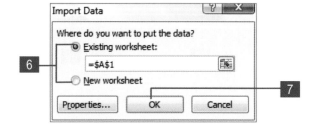

Data is only valuable when it's current, and simply inserting information from a query into a worksheet doesn't mean that it's the latest available data. Data changes constantly on the web. As it changes you can use the Refresh button to update the data – as long as you are online, of course.

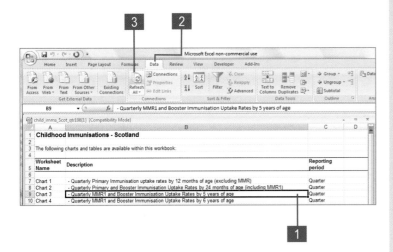

1. Click any cell in the worksheet that contains the query data.

2. Click the **Data** tab.

3. Click the **Refresh** button. The query is performed again and, after the remote website is connected, the data is refreshed.

?

Did you know?

Obviously, you need to be online in order to refresh data from the web. While the query is being performed, the circular refresh icon spins to tell you the query is running. If it seems to be spinning too long, you can double-click this icon to check the status of the query.

9

Editing a query

The process of retrieving a saved query is relatively simple. But if you want to edit a query, some additional steps are involved. However, if you haven't saved a query and need to make a slight adjustment to the URL or another change, editing a query is easier than searching for the web page and copying the address through a search engine.

1 Open the file that contains the data you want to update.

2 Click the **Data** tab.

3 Click **Connections**.

4 Click **Properties**.

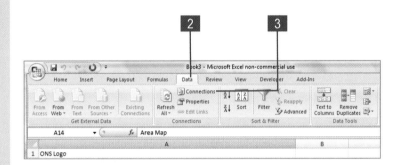

5 Click the **Definition** tab.

6 Click **Edit Query**.

7 When the New Web Query dialogue box opens, adjust the URL or click **Options** to change the query.

8 Click **Go** (or press [Enter]) to perform the query with the new criteria.

9

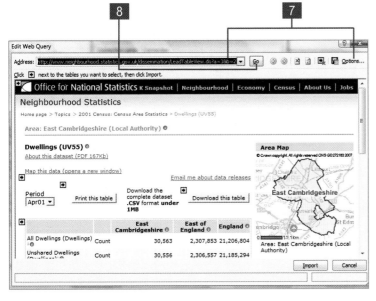

Making external links

▶

When you import data from a web query, you see that many of the cells contain hypertext links. Click on one of the links, and you realise that it is 'live' – a web browser opens, and it connects to the page referenced in the hyperlink. You can make hypertext links within an Excel 2007 worksheet, just as you can from within other Microsoft Office applications. Each link can be to another place in the same file, to another file on your local file system, or to a remote location on the internet.

1 Click the cell that you want to contain the hyperlink.

2 Click the **Insert** tab.

3 Click **Hyperlink** in the Links group.

Making an internal hyperlink

4 When the Insert Hyperlink dialogue box appears, under Link to list on the left, click **Place in This Document**. When you click Place in this Document, the options in the dialogue box change, as shown in the adjacent screen.

5 Click here to link to Sheet3 in your workbook.

6 In the Text to display box, type the text that will be visible as a link.

7 Click **ScreenTip** to enter some text that will appear as a screen tip when the user mouses over the link.

8 Click **OK**.

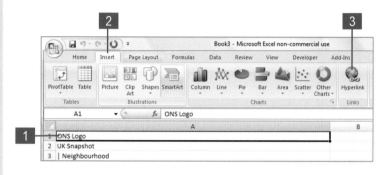

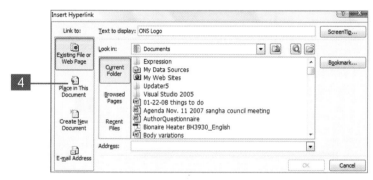

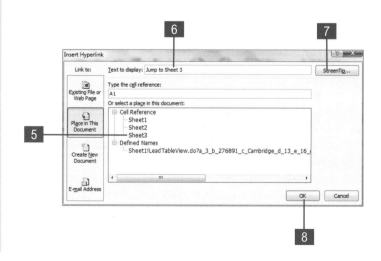

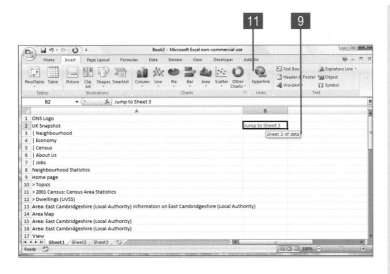

Making an external hyperlink

9 When the link appears, mouse over it and check for the screen tip to make sure it's accurate.

10 Click the cell that you want to contain the hyperlink.

11 Click **Insert Hyperlink**.

12 Click **Existing File or Web Page**.

13 Type the visible text for the hyperlink.

14 Type the web address for the hyperlink.

15 Click **OK**.

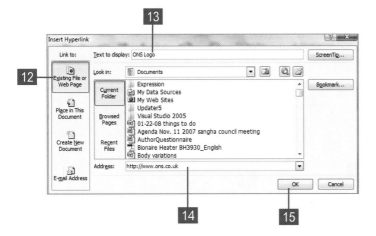

Did you know?

You can also make an external link that isn't on the web. Rather, the link goes to another workbook on your computer. Click **Existing File or Web Page** under Link to. Locate the workbook on your file system and double-click it to select it. You return to Insert Hyperlink dialogue box, where you can type the clickable text and a screen tip if you want one.

Retrieving data with the Web Data Add-In

1. Click the **Data** tab.
2. Click the **down arrow** just beneath From Web, and choose Advanced Mode.
3. Type the web address of the site you want to connect to.
4. Use the navigation buttons to browse the site, much like a web browser.

When you click the From Web button on the Data to make a Web Query, two options appear. The first option was covered in preceding tasks. It's easy to overlook the second option, Advanced Mode. When you click Advanced Mode, the Web Data Add-In opens. At first glance, this add-in seems very similar to the other option, the usual New Web Query dialogue box. It's even called New Web Query. But in my experience, there are some differences. One big difference: the advanced option operates more quickly than New Web Query. Also, the advanced option works much like a web browser. There are navigations at the top that help you browse for information on a remote website, which is particularly helpful if you don't yet know the web address of the site you want.

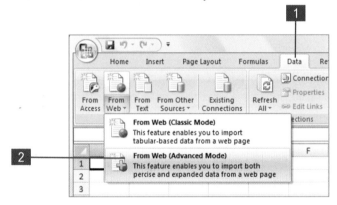

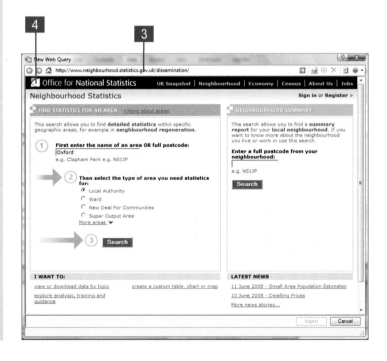

Retrieving data with the Web Data Add-In (cont.)

5

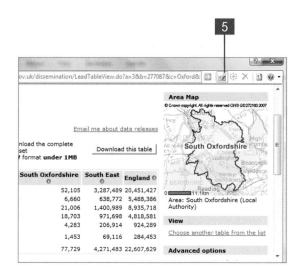

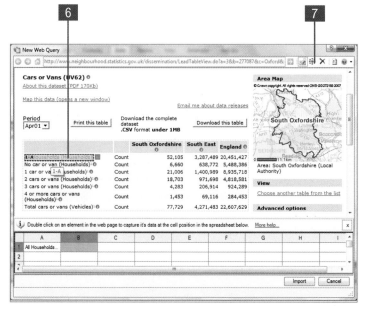

5 When you see the data you want, click **Capture Data**.

A small spreadsheet opens in the bottom half of New Web Query.

6 Mouse over some data, and notice that a red box appears around the cell. Double-click the cell, and the contents are added to the spreadsheet below.

7 Click **Select Similar**, and Excel will automatically make similar selections based on your previous ones.

9

Sharing your Excel data

Introduction

Excel is one of several applications that you can use to connect and work with a site that uses Microsoft Office SharePoint® technology. SharePoint is an environment that helps individuals and workgroups collaborate online. By combining Excel and SharePoint, you are able to track and chart data with a new level of sophistication, and share your work with colleagues anywhere in the world. In this chapter, you'll learn about the many ways Excel and SharePoint can combine to provide easier access to data than ever before.

What you'll do

Install the Microsoft Office Live add-in

Access a document workspace from within Excel

Publish an Excel document to a document workspace

Work with the Document Management task pane

Export list content to Excel

Create a document workspace from within Excel

Working with Excel Services

Options for collaborating with other Excel users

Most people don't use Excel in a vacuum. If you use Excel in the workplace, chances are you use it to prepare reports, which you share with your supervisors or co-workers. You probably also need to make your Excel workbooks available to others within your organisation. You can, of course, simply email your files to your co-workers. If you are on the same local computer network (a network within a single facility) you can post your Excel files on the file server, and those who have permission can access the files and work with them.

But these days, organisations have many different branches. I have a friend who works with Excel to prepare sophisticated chemical reports. She works in one Illinois town. The corporate headquarters is in downtown Chicago. There are branches in Georgia and other states. How do those users open files securely, view and edit them, and put them back where co-workers can find them and add their own changes? The internet is the obvious solution.

Excel, in fact, is ideally configured to store and access files published to online storage areas called document workspaces. A document workspace can be found in one of two places:

- on a computer that runs file sharing and collaboration software called Microsoft Office SharePoint Server® (MOSS);

- on an office collaboration site that Microsoft makes available to individuals and businesses, called Microsoft Office Live.

SharePoint is a sophisticated environment that requires an organisation to install and maintain server software. Office Live is more accessible to individuals, and while both options will be discussed in this chapter, Office Live will get the most attention. But Office Live makes use of SharePoint technology, so if you learn how to use Office Live, you'll gain familiarity with SharePoint as well.

One of your first questions regarding collaboration sites such as Office Live and SharePoint is likely to be: how do I connect them with Microsoft Excel? Since Office Live and SharePoint are web-based services, you can access both with a web browser, as long as you have an account and are an authorised user. With SharePoint, you need to obtain a username and password through your network administrator. Office Live is more of a do-it-yourself operation. After you obtain an Office Live account, the next step to connect Excel and Office Live is to install the Office Live add-in. It's part of a package called the Office Live update.

1 Go to the Microsoft Download Center, **http://www.microsoft.com/ downloads**, and search for Office Live Update.

2 When the download page for this program appears, click the **Download** button.

3 Click **Run**.

10

Installing the Microsoft Office Live add-in (cont.)

4 When a User Account Control dialogue box appears, click **Continue**.

5 Follow the steps required to install the Office Live Update software.

6 Restart your computer.

7 Once the system has restarted, open Excel and click the **Office** button.

8 Make sure the new Office Live options are available: click the Office button and look for the two new **Office** Live options.

For your information

It's free to sign up for Office Live and to use the document workspace feature. You need to set up a Windows Live ID. To get started, go to the Office Live home page, **http://www.officelive.com/default.aspx**, and click the **Sign Up Free** button under Office Live Workspaces.

Once you have signed up for an account with Office Live Workspace and have installed the add-in, you can access a workspace in one of two ways: from Office Live itself with your web browser, or from Excel. If your goal is to copy a file from the workspace to an Excel file so you can chart it or print it, the easier option is from Excel. Just follow these steps.

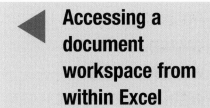

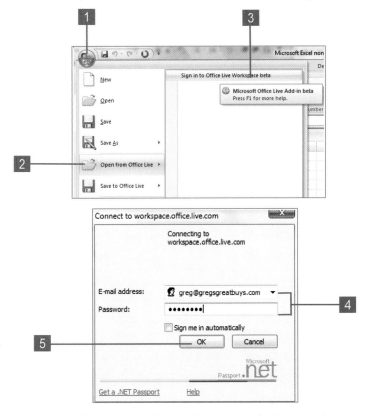

1 Click the **Office** button.

2 Point to Open from Office Live.

3 Click **Sign in to Office Live Workspace**.

4 Type your Windows Live ID or .NET username and password.

5 Click **OK**.

6 Click **Documents**.

10

Accessing a
document
workspace from
within Excel (cont.)

7 When the list of files in the
document workspace appears,
click the file you want to
download.

8 Click **Open**.

9 The file opens in Excel in a
read-only version within a
larger Excel window.

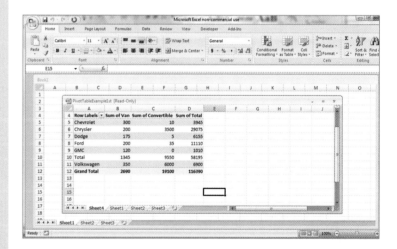

Once you are able to establish a connection between Excel 2007 and a document workspace, it becomes an easy matter to publish an Excel file to a document workspace. That way, other users who have permission to access the workspace can view and edit the file. The only problem is one of security; you need to make sure the files you publish are ones that can be shared with other users.

Publishing an Excel document to a document workspace

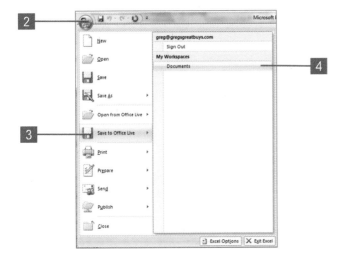

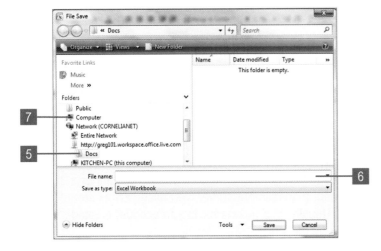

1 Edit and save the Excel worksheet you want to publish to the document workspace.

2 Click the **Office** button.

3 Point to Save to Office Live.

4 If you are already signed in to the workspace, the options are different from those shown in the preceding task. Click **Documents** under the heading Workspace.

5 Notice that the File Save dialogue box opens with the destination, the Docs folder in the document workspace, selected.

6 If you know the path leading to the file (for example, C\Excel Files\Customer_List.xls), type it here.

7 If you don't know the path, click the **down arrow** next to Computer and browse until you locate the file you want.

10

Publishing an Excel document to a document workspace (cont.)

8 Click the file when you locate it, so its name is listed in the File Name box.

9 Scroll down the list of folders and resources on the left side of the File Save dialogue box until you locate the **Docs** file, and click it. When you click the Docs folder, the workspace appears on the right-hand side of the File Save dialogue box.

10 Click **Save**. A progress dialogue box appears briefly to let you know the file has been saved.

To check whether the file has actually been saved to the workspace, follow the steps in the next task.

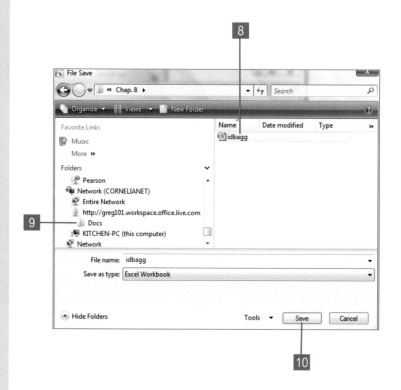

When you use Excel to open a file stored in a document workspace on a SharePoint or Office Live server, the Document Management task pane should open automatically. This task pane's controls enable you to manage files on the remote server. If the task pane does not open automatically, you can do it manually as shown below.

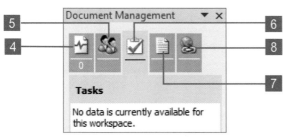

1 Click the **Office** button.

2 Point to Server.

3 Choose Document Management Information. The Document Management task pane opens.

4 Click here to view any lists that have been published in the workspace.

5 Click here to view any members who have access to the workspace.

6 Click here to view any tasks – lists of things to do – that have been created for those who use the workspace.

7 Click here to view a list of documents in the workspace.

8 Click here to view any links that have been made for this workspace.

10

For your information

The Server option only appears under the Office menu if the currently active document has a connection to a remote server such as a SharePoint or Office Live site. Other open Excel files that don't have such a connection won't have the Server option visible.

Exporting list content to Excel

A document workspace site also provides lists that help your team to communicate and track tasks, such as announcements and links. For example, you might want to introduce a new team member who is working on the project or share a link to a related website. You can also sign up to get alerts for the document or the workspace, so that you receive an email message when someone changes a document or adds new content.

Create a List

1 With your web browser, log in to your Office Live document workspace site.

2 Click the **down arrow** next to New and choose List, or one of the more specific options: Task List, Contact List, or Event List. (For this example, choose Contact List.)

3 Click in each of the boxes beneath the headings First Name, Last Name, and so on, and type the contact information.

4 Click **Add Row** to add new names as needed.

Exporting the list

5 When you're done, click **Save**.

6 Click **Export to Excel**.

7 If this warning bar appears, click it and choose Download File.

8 After the necessary software has downloaded, click **Export to Excel** again.

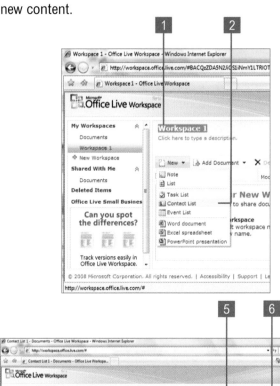

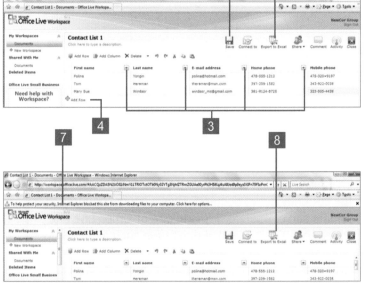

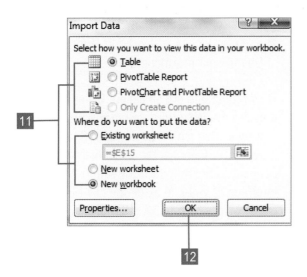

9 Click **Open**.

10 If a security dialogue box appears, click **Enable**.

11 When the Import Data dialogue box appears, choose the form you want the data to take, and whether it should be saved in a new worksheet or new workbook.

12 Click **OK**.

10

What is Microsoft SharePoint?

Microsoft Office SharePoint® is a server technology that allows individuals or groups in different locations to collaborate on projects and share information by means of a server running SharePoint server software. SharePoint is designed to help organisations design workflows and stay competitive by sharing up to the minute information.

One of SharePoint's many advantages is its degree of integration with Microsoft Excel. Excel document types are recognised by SharePoint, for one thing. But more than that, you can use Excel to:

- query a SharePoint list;
- print out SharePoint data with Excel;

- create charts with Excel using the information on a SharePoint-managed site;
- and even create a PivotTable report using SharePoint information.

These functions are all called 'Office Links', and they are available from within the SharePoint interface. This isn't a book about SharePoint, however. In this chapter, you'll learn how to connect to SharePoint from within the Excel interface. If you use a service like Microsoft Office Live, which is based in part on SharePoint technology, you'll be able to import Excel information and export data to Excel, too.

Working with Excel Web Access

Excel Web Access is one of the two primary methods (along with Excel Services, described below) that enable you to move data between Excel worksheets and SharePoint sites. When you save to SharePoint as HTML, for instance, Web Access opens automatically and turns the spreadsheet into an HTML document. Once the spreadsheet is open in a web browser, you can give others a link and they can view it without your having to send them the actual document.

Excel Web Access is a web page component called a Web Part. It allows you to connect to an Excel workbook from within a web browser. The Excel Web Access Web Part (that's its formal name) presents Excel spreadsheet information on a Web Part page. The result looks very much like the usual Excel workbook, in fact.

If you have access to SharePoint, Office Live, or another collaborative environment, the most obvious way to create a document workspace is to connect to it with your web browser and use the web-based interface. But if you have been given an account to access the collaborative environment by your network administrator, you also have the ability to save some time by creating the workspace within Excel. You have two options: use the Document Management task pane or send an email message.

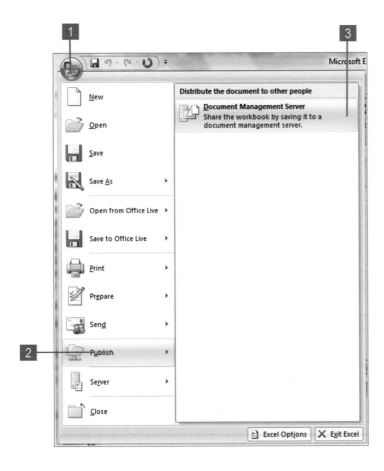

 Creating a document workspace from within Excel

Using the Document Management task pane

1 Click the **Office** button.

2 Point to Publish.

3 Choose Document Management Server.

10

Creating a document workspace from within Excel (cont.)

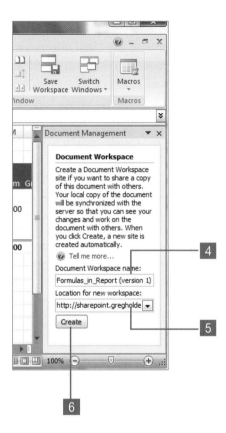

4 In the Document Management task pane, type a name for your workspace.

5 In the Location for new workspace list, enter the location of the SharePoint site where you want to create the workspace.

6 Click **Create**.

7 Click **Yes** when you are prompted to save the file.

Did you know?

As long as you have a connection to your document workspace, you can refresh the information stored there. If one of your colleagues publishes a new file to the workspace, for instance, refreshing it will allow you to see it and download it so you can work with it. Click the **Get Updates** button at the bottom of the Document Management workspace to refresh the connection.

192

Working with Excel Services

In order to start using Excel Services, you need to create an Excel worksheet or workbook. You then load the file into Excel Services, which means you make the data in the file available through SharePoint. Excel Services then lets you perform familiar Excel tools, such as:

- calculation
- charts
- data connections
- dates
- Excel tables
- functions
- names
- 'what if' analysis.

Some Excel 2007 features are not supported by Excel Services. These include comments, controls for form toolbars, data validation, digital signatures, displayed formulas, queries, shared workbooks and VBA code.

10

Beginning VBA

Introduction

If you're reading this book, you are probably curious about one of Excel's most powerful features: the ability to execute tasks using Visual Basic® for Applications, or VBA for short. VBA is a version of the Visual Basic programming language that runs exclusively within the framework of specific Microsoft programs. VBA is a less robust version of VB, which can be used to create executable software components. (Another member of the VB family, VBScript, is designed specifically for use in web pages.)

If the idea of programming is a terrifying prospect for you, then fear not. VBA is arguably the easiest language out there to learn and use, and with a little practice you'll be enhancing your Excel use in no time. In fact, VBA was one of the primary features that led to Excel's dominant position in the spreadsheet market. Functions written in VBA are widely used throughout both the public and private sectors.

There are a few ways to start working with VBA, all of which will be covered in this chapter. You will see why it's become so popular, since you can start working with VBA code without even knowing the basic syntax by recording a macro, which we'll also do in this chapter. You'll also see that you've already worked with VBA earlier in the book, whether you were aware of it or not, simply by creating data forms, for example.

One thing to remember when learning to use VBA in Excel is that VBA, like all programming languages, has a syntax, and a glossary of terms that you'll need to familiarise yourself with as

What you'll do

Record a macro as a way of learning VBA

Work with the Visual Basic Editor

Reference ranges vs. reference cells

Declare variables

Add comments to VBA code

you advance. Luckily, this information is widely available online. A great place to start is the WikiBooks Visual Basic/Getting Started entry at:

http://en.wikibooks.org/wiki/Visual_Basic/Getting_Started

Among other things, it includes a list of the Reserved Words in VBA, terms that are used as specific functions and commands, such as And, As, True, False, etc. You can also find a very helpful VBA Glossary at this address:

http://www.csidata.com/custserv/onlinehelp/vbsdocs/vbs0.htm

The primary goal of this chapter is to get your feet wet so that you're comfortable in the interface and have a basic understanding of where things are. You'll also receive an introduction to key concepts on which you can start building your knowledge.

Microsoft Excel has many powerful tools available to you through a few simple clicks of the mouse. It would be impossible, however, for software developers to anticipate every custom application that a user might dream up. This is where VBA code comes into play. Suppose you want to create a user form that has a particular set of buttons and dropdowns and changes one custom image to another when the task is completed, but that is dependent on a particular set of data that was generated from your company. Of course, there won't be any tool to perform that exact function, but if you know VBA, you can write the code yourself. Because you can use VBA to automate tasks, you will quickly see how it makes your experience with Excel more efficient.

Microsoft introduced Visual Basic for Applications (VBA) in 1993, and since then it has become widely used across virtually every sector of the business world and many other fields as well. It is an event-driven programming language, meaning that the program flow is determined by the user (or by sensor outputs), as opposed to batch programming, where the flow is determined by the programmer.

VBA is a component of all Office applications, and most Microsoft applications more generally. Moreover, it has become so widespread that it is implemented into prominent third-party software such as AutoCAD, WordPerfect and ArcGIS.

It should be pointed out that VBA distribution licences to new customers ceased to be available as of 1 July 2007 and, as of February 2008, extended support for VBA has been discontinued. This is because Microsoft is making the somewhat controversial transition of its products to a new language, Visual Basic.NET. That said, learning VBA provides a basic foundation on which you can transition to more sophisticated languages if you wish, and the fact that VBA is so ingrained in so many industries means that you can expect to encounter VBA code for years to come.

Recording a macro as a way of learning VBA

1. Open a blank Excel workbook.
2. Click the **Developer** tab.
3. Click **Record** Macro.
4. The Record Macro dialogue will appear. Give it the name, Sample1.
5. Check this box to store the macro in This Workbook.

   You don't really need to assign a shortcut key at this time.
6. Click **OK**.

   You should see a record button, and the text, Stop Recording, where Record Macro was before. The macro is now recording.

For many people who have never programmed before, the natural first question arises: 'Where, exactly, do I program?' Because VBA is built directly into Excel 2007, it's easy to create or modify code, and recording a macro is the easiest way of all. This method allows you to record a series of events as code that you can then run as a macro whenever you want, allowing you to automate your task. This is also a great way for beginners to learn VBA, because you can record macros and then examine the code generated to see how VBA code accomplishes particular tasks.

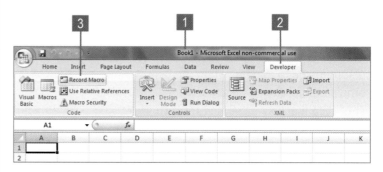

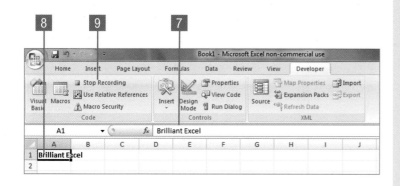

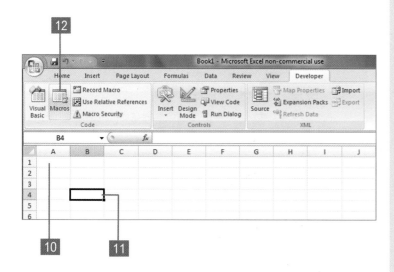

7 Type 'Brilliant Excel' into cell A1, and click on the cell.

8 Select the text by scrolling across it, and press [Ctrl]+[B] to format the text in bold.

9 Click **Stop Recording**.

You've just created your first macro, and created VBA code as well.

10 Delete the text from cell A1.

11 Click any empty cell in the worksheet to make the ribbon buttons active.

12 To run your macro, click on the **Macros** icon in the Code group.

Recording a macro as a way of learning VBA (cont.)

13 In the dialogue box, Sample1 should be the only macro name available because that's all you've created so far.

14 Click **Run**, and the text should reappear in cell A1.

15 To see the code that you created, select Edit from the Macros dialogue. The Microsoft Visual Basic application window will open, and a module containing the code you created will appear.

16 Now you can study the code to get a sense of how certain commands are carried out, as described in the next task.

See also

Macros do represent a potential security risk, and in Chapter 8 you learn how to adjust Excel's security settings to protect yourself against malicious code that can be inserted into macros that you download. Chapter 15 also examines macros as timesavers rather than as tools for working with VBA.

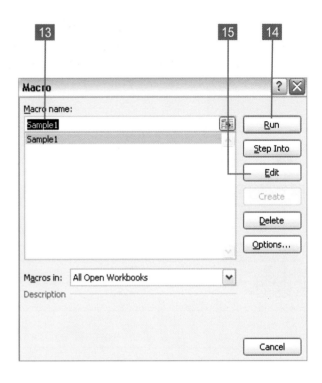

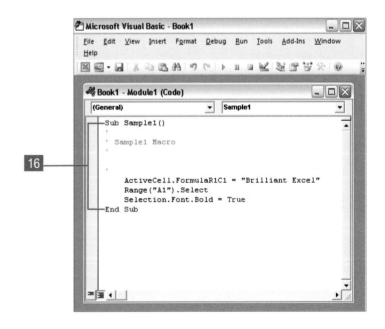

200

The interface that you entered at the end of the preceding task is called the Visual Basic Editor. In this editing window you can write, edit and modify VBA code. The Visual Basic Editor allows you to view your project in many different ways.

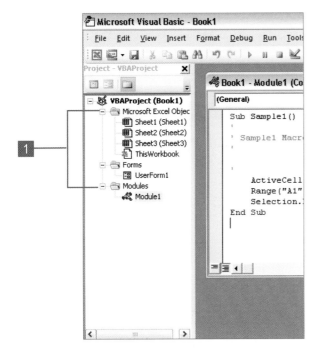

Did you know?

Another way to access the editor is by clicking on the **Visual Basic** icon in the Code group on the Developer tab.

1 Click the **Project Explorer** icon on the toolbar to bring up a tree chart on the left-hand side showing you the different types of folders that are available.

You'll see three kinds of folder available: Microsoft Excel Objects, Forms and Modules.

- Microsoft Excel Objects: These are your workbooks. If you added an additional sheet to your Excel file, you would see a fourth sheet appear in the Microsoft Excel Objects folder.

- Forms: These are the user forms that we introduced in the chapter on data forms. As you remember, you create the layout for user forms in the Microsoft Visual Basic Editor, and then use VBA code to tell them what to do.

- Modules: This is where functions written in VBA code are stored. Note that the macro you created is a module.

Referencing ranges vs. referencing cells

One of the easiest ways you can begin to work with VBA is to edit the references made to cells or ranges of cells. By changing a single cell reference to a range, you enlarge the amount of data the code affects. You just need to be careful that the values you enter exactly match the ranges and cells you want to work with.

1 Examine the VBA code generated by the first task once again. You'll notice that the second line reads:

```
Range ("A1").Select
```

The module you created references the range at the intersection of column A and row 1, a range which, in this case, consists of only a single cell. This is how macros are recorded: they use standard Excel notation (i.e. column and row) to designate cells. For this reason, they are ideal for VBA code where you want to perform a function on a range of cells. In the steps that follow, you'll reference cells using the Range command to assign a particular font to the text across multiple cells.

2 Close the module, Sample1, by clicking the **Close** box.

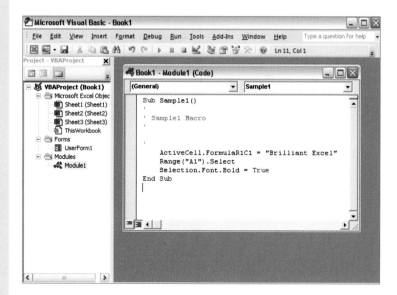

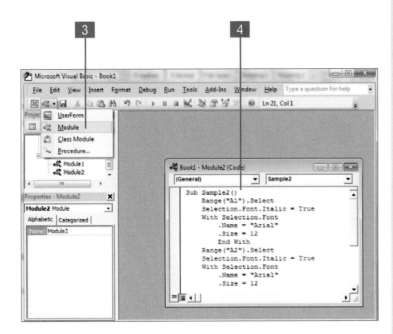

3
Open a new module by clicking the **Insert UserForm down arrow** between the Excel logo and the Save icon in the Visual Basic Editor and choosing Module from the drop-down list.

4
Enter the following code into the new Module:

```
Sub Sample2()
 Range("A1").Select
Selection.Font.Italic
= True
 With Selection.Font
    .Name = "Arial"
    .Size = 12
    End With
 Range("A2").Select
Selection.Font.Italic
= True
 With Selection.Font
    .Name = "Arial"
    .Size = 12
    End With
    Range("A3").Select
Selection.Font.Italic
= True
 With Selection.Font
    .Name = "Arial"
    .Size = 12
    End With
End Sub
```

Referencing ranges vs. referencing cells (cont.)

5 Now go back to your Excel Sheet1 and type any text you want in cells A1, A2, and A3.

6 Click the **green triangle** in the Visual Basic Editor (the Run button).

If you copied the code correctly, your text should become italicised, formatted to font size 12, and rendered to Arial font type.

The next type of referencing that you're going to see has many inherent advantages of its own. Referencing a cell instead of a range allows you to create a loop, which is code that can repeat an action as often as you instruct it to. As you become more familiar with Excel, you'll realise the value of being able to automate your worksheets in such a way; looping is one of the most useful features that VBA adds to Excel.

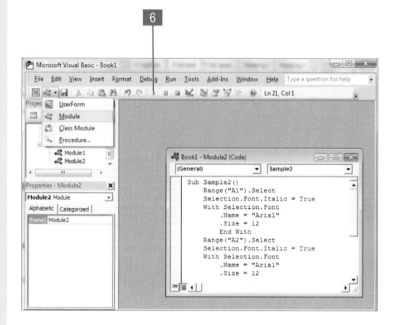

7 Enter the following code into the very same module you just created:

```
Sub Sample3()
 For x = 1 To 10
   Cells(x, 1).Select
   Selection.Value =
 x + 1
 Next x
End Sub
```

Notice that the Visual Basic Editor automatically separates the commands between End Sub and Sub to create two independent functions.

8 Go to Sheet2, and click the **Run** button in the Visual Basic Editor. The numbers 2 through 11 should appear in column A. Unlike when referencing a range, referencing a cell identifies the column first, then the row. In this case, you've identified the column as whatever x happens to be, and the row as 1, causing your code to run from cell A1 through A10, commensurate with the increasing value of x. The reason why it's called a loop is because it executes a command on the value produced by the previous command, which is a key element of automating actions.

Declaring variables

This next task will show you the power of declaring variables to streamline your code. Not only does declaring variables make it easier to tell what's going on, it can also help to avoid confusion and code errors down the line.

Examine the code you wrote for the example where you referenced a range. To produce the desired result, it was necessary to copy essentially the same code over three times, once for each cell on which you wanted it to run. Declaring variables allows you to specify the nature of an object in your code so that you can simply change the nature of that object instead of having to keep retyping code that's virtually identical over and over again. This should make more sense when you have a look at the code.

1 Type the following code into the same module where you typed the original range referencing example so you can look at them both at once:

```
Sub Sample2()
Dim RNG As Range
Set RNG =
Range("A1:A8")
   With RNG.Font
      .Name = "Arial"
      .Size = 12
      .Italic = True
   End With
End Sub
```

Running this code should produce the exact same effect as the first code you wrote, but this time, see how you defined the variable, RNG, as a range, and you can now set it to be whatever you want. This is much more convenient (and reliable because it helps to avoid typos), and more efficient as well. Dim stands for Dimension; what you've done here is also known as 'dimensioning'.

There's one more very important thing to remember when you're writing code: leave notes! Adding comments to code is the key to having code that does what it's supposed to do going forward, and is easier to debug if need be because you'll remember what it was that you *wanted* it to do.

To add comments to VBA code, you simply insert a ['] or the letters REM before each line of commentary to instruct the program not to treat this as active code. Now you'll add some commentary to the code you just wrote.

For your information

Lastly, remember that if you place an apostrophe in front of an actual line of code, that code will not run.

1 You can write anything you want, but here's an example of good commenting:

```
Sub Sample2()
Dim RNG As Range
' **********
' Here, I can set
the range to
whatever cells I
want
' **********
Set RNG =
Range("A1:A8")
  With RNG.Font
    .Name ="Arial"
    .Size = 12
    .Italic = True
  End With
End Sub
```

The asterisks have been included just as a visual indicator. While they aren't necessary, you'll quickly find that they can be very helpful when parsing long strings of code.

Customising the interface

Introduction

Excel 2007 has a complex and rich interface, but to long-time users of Excel and other Office programs, it's a little unfamiliar. You're probably used to having a selection of toolbars and menus instead of the ribbon, for instance. You can still make the interface suit your working habits, however. You can also personalise the application so that elements you use frequently are easier to find. Once you do make changes, it's easy to undo them and restore default arrangements as needed. In this chapter, you'll learn simple tips and approaches that will enable you to customise Excel so that it works the way you want.

What you'll do

View Excel's tool groups

Customise the fill handle

Add a custom document property

Customise a cell's style

Customise workbook views

Create a custom header

Make a custom template

Add custom colours to a worksheet

Add a scroll bar to a worksheet

Can you customise the ribbon?

The ribbon is part of the Microsoft Office Fluent user interface. By default, the ribbon is optimised for a screen resolution of 1024 × 768 pixels. The ribbon is subdivided into individual tabs (Home, Insert, etc.). Each of those tabs, in turn, is subdivided into groups of tools. (For instance, the Home tab contains the Clipboard group of tools, the Font group, the Alignment group, and so on.)

If you minimise the Excel window (in other words, make it smaller than your current screen size), the icons shown change, too. Instead of all the icons, you see placeholders for groups of icons. For instance, if the Excel window is maximised so it takes up your entire screen space, you see all of the Font tools.

But if you minimise the window by dragging the left or right edge towards the center, you see a placeholder for the Font group.

If you click the **down arrow** beneath the Font placeholder, you see the rest of the tools:

You have less control over what appears on the ribbon than you did in previous versions of Excel, which allowed you to customise each of the toolbars and menus. With the ribbon, real customisation only comes as a result of programming the interface using eXtensible Markup Language (XML) or Visual Basic. It's a complex prospect that, in some cases, involves installing some software utilities. (If you're interested in changing the interface with a utility called the UI Editor, go to **http://www.rondebruin.nl/ribbon.htm**. To customise the ribbon with XML, go to **http://msdn.microsoft.com/en-us/library/aa338202.aspx**.) If you're not experienced with such programming languages, by doing this kind of work you run the risk of damaging the application.

What can you do to change the ribbon? Not much. Microsoft specifically says you can't add or remove tools without programming, and you can't switch to old-style toolbar and menu arrangements. You can only use the Quick Access Toolbar, which you can customise freely.

In previous versions of Excel, you were given 'short' and 'long' versions. When you first clicked on a menu, you saw the short version – the commands Excel thought you were most likely to use, because you had used them in the past. If you clicked on a down arrow, you saw the 'long' version with the full set of tools. In Excel 2007, instead of menus, you have the ribbon, its tabs, and its tool groups. But you might not realise at first that many tool groups have 'short' and 'long' versions, too, and the 'long' version enables you to perform functions you couldn't do with the ribbon alone.

Viewing Excel's tool groups

1. Suppose you want to indent a block of text or a set of data. Click the **Home** tab.

2. Click the **small arrow** in the lower right-hand corner of the Alignment tool group.

3. Click the alignment options you want.

4. Click **OK**.

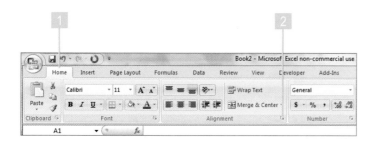

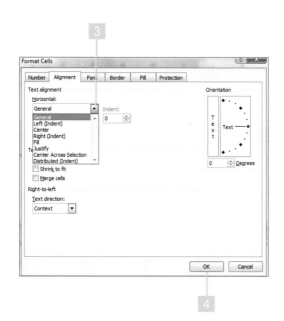

For your information

When you are looking for a command that doesn't appear in the ribbon by default, such as Tabs, it pays to look at the Customize section of Excel Options. (Click the **Office** button, click **Excel Options**, and click Customize.) You see commands that you can add to the Quick Access Toolbar. Search through each of the tabs in the ribbon, and you'll find lots of commands you didn't even know you had. You won't find a Tab command, but you do see Tab Color, Sum, Text that Contains…, and many other unusual options.

Customising the fill handle

The fill handle in the bottom right corner of a cell lets you automatically continue a series of numbers or text strings. But you can customise the fill handle to automatically add a list of your own creation. First, you create the list. Then, you add the list to the fill handle in Excel Options either by typing it on the spot, or by importing it from a range of cells. Finally, you drag the fill handle to add the list to your workbook.

Type the custom list

1 Click the **Office** button.

2 Click **Excel Options** to open the Excel Options dialogue box.

3 Click **Popular**.

4 Click **Edit Custom Lists...**

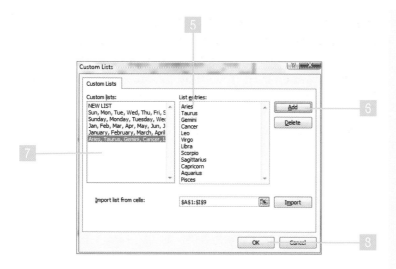

5 When the Custom Lists dialogue box opens, type the list in List entries.

6 Click **Add**.

7 The new list appears in the Custom Lists window.

8 Click **OK** to close Custom Lists, and **OK** to close the Customise window.

Add the custom list

9 Click on the cell where you want the list to start.

Did you know?

You can also import a custom fill list from a spreadsheet. Select the cells in your spreadsheet that contain the list elements by dragging across them. Once you select the cells, follow the steps shown in this task. The range of cells you selected will be displayed in the Import list from cells box at the bottom of the Custom Lists dialogue box. Click **Import**, and the list will be imported.

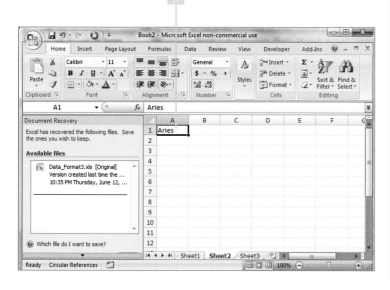

Customising the
fill handle (cont.)

10 Type the first name in the list.

11 Press [Enter].

12 Click on the cell containing the first name in the list.

13 Click and hold down the mouse pointer on the fill handle in the bottom right-hand corner of the active cell.

14 Drag the fill handle to auto fill as many cells as needed. Notice that a ScreenTip appears to indicate the next item that will be added in the series.

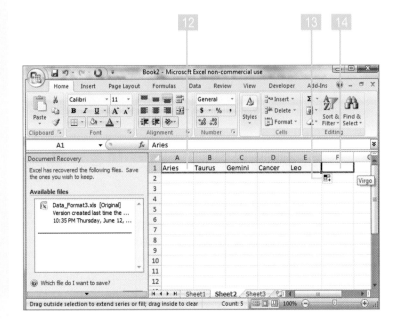

Document properties, or metadata, can help you manage files based on the criteria they contain. When you enter a title, subject, author, category or other document property, a search engine can find your file more easily. By creating a custom property, you provide more specific information that a search engine can use to find the file more easily.

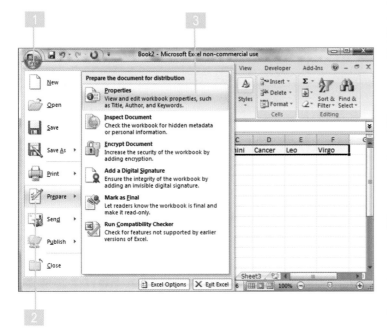

1 Click the **Office** button.

2 Point to Prepare.

3 Choose Properties.

4 Click the **down arrow** next to Document Properties.

5 Click **Advanced Properties**.

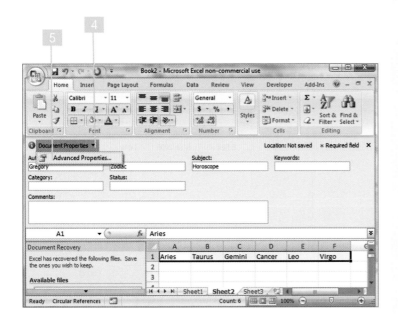

Adding a custom document property (cont.)

6 Click the tabs in Advanced Properties to add information about the file:

- General lets you add size or location details.

- Summary lets you add title and author information.

- Statistics lets you display the number of slides, words, or other details.

7 Click **Custom**.

8 Type a name for the custom property, or select an option from the list beneath the Name box.

9 Specify the type of the property.

10 Type a value for the property.

11 Click **Add**.

12 Click **OK**.

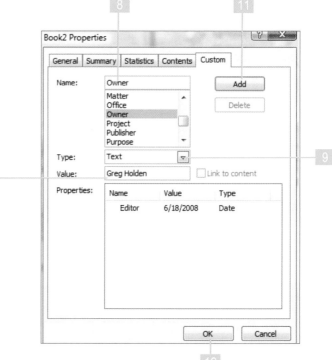

You might not think a cell has a style. That's because the colour, type font, and other visual attributes that a cell can have are not always something you think about. After all, you are preoccupied with entering and working with data. But cells do have a selection of formatting instructions that, together, constitute a style. If you save the style with a name, you can easily move the style from one cell or one worksheet to another. Styles can make data easier to interpret. For instance, you can have all totals show up in 14-point Helvetica with a blue background, and all dollar amounts that are over budget in red 18-point Arial, and so on. What's more, Excel makes the process of assigning styles especially easy by providing you with a set of built-in styles you can apply. Once you assign a style to a cell, you can prevent others from changing it by locking the cell.

1 Select the cell or cells to which you want to apply formatting.

2 Click the **Home** tab.

3 Click **Cell Styles**.

4 Click **New Cell Style**.

5 When the Style dialogue box opens, type a name for the style you want to create.

6 Click the **Format** button.

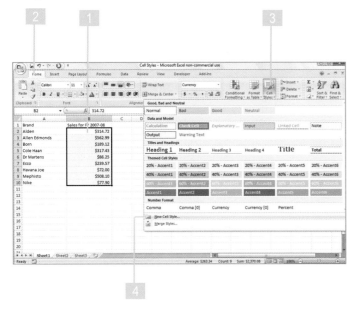

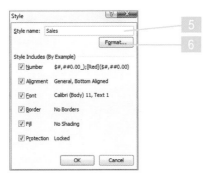

Customising a cell's style (cont.)

7

7 When the Format Cells dialogue box opens, apply the formatting you want, based on the options available on each of the six tabs. For example:

- On the Number tab, specify the form in which numerals are to be presented. You can specify whether to use the pounds or euros symbol before numerals, for instance.

- On the Alignment tab, you can choose whether to align text vertically or horizontally.

- The Font tab gives you common text controls, such as the font name, size and colour.

- On the Border tab, you can choose a line to place around each cell, and whether the border should be assigned a colour.

- The Fill tab allows you to fill the contents of the cell with a colour.

- On the Protection tab, you can specify whether the selected cells' contents should be locked or hidden, which can be useful if the workbook will be shared with others who might have the chance to edit it.

Customising a cell's style (cont.)

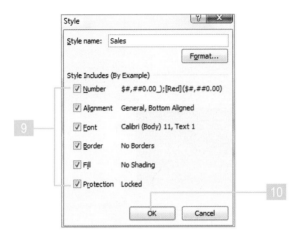

8 When you're done formatting, click **OK**.

The Format Cells dialogue box closes and you return to Style.

9 Uncheck any boxes for formatting you don't want to apply.

10 Click **OK** to close the Style dialogue box and return to your worksheet.

11 Click **Cell Styles** to view the new style in the Cell Styles gallery.

12 Right-click the style name and choose Modify to edit it.

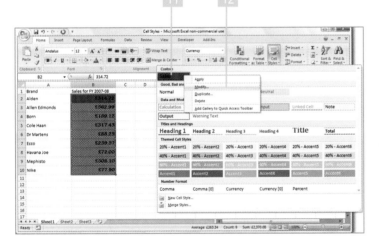

For your information

This overrides any formatting you may have applied in Format Cells, so be careful. If you have applied a fill in the Fill tab of Format Cells and then uncheck the Fill box in Style, you won't have any fills in your cells.

Customising workbook views

Any Excel workbook can be assigned settings that determine how it is displayed and printed. You can create custom workbook views for different purposes. For instance, one custom view can determine how a workbook behaves when it is opened and another can determine the print area, for example.

1 Create your workbook so it is formatted with the view and print settings you want.

2 Click the **View** tab.

3 Click **Custom Views**.

4 Click **Add**.

5 Type a name for the custom view you want to create.

6 Check or uncheck the Print settings or Hidden rows, columns and filter settings boxes.

7 Click **OK**.

A header is a label that gives an official look to your worksheet. It serves much the same purpose as a header or footer in a Microsoft Word word processing file. It can contain the name of the worksheet, the logo of your company and your own name, among other things. Instead of using the Page Setup dialogue box as in previous versions, in Excel 2007 you use the View tab to create a header.

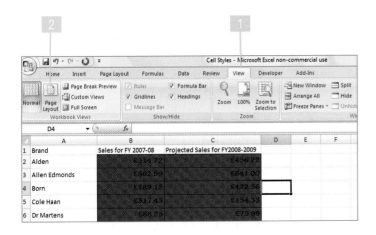

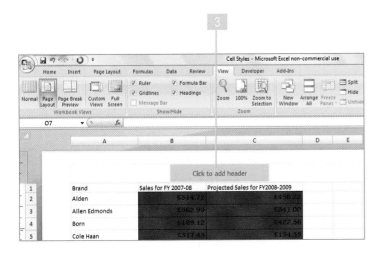

Creating a custom header

1 Click the **View** tab.

2 Click **Page Layout**.

3 Click the words **Click to add header** to highlight them.

12

Creating a custom header (cont.)

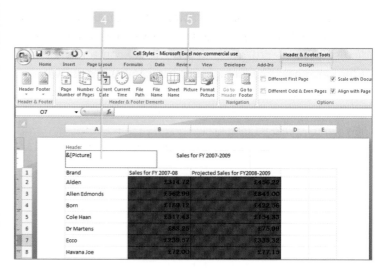

4 Click in the box to the left of the header you just typed.

5 Click **Picture** to add a logo. The placeholder &[Picture] is added.

6 Click in any cell, and the visual image appears.

7 Click in the left-hand header box where you just added the image.

8 Click **Format Picture** in the Header & Footer Tools ribbon. Adjust the settings in the Format Picture dialogue box and click **OK**.

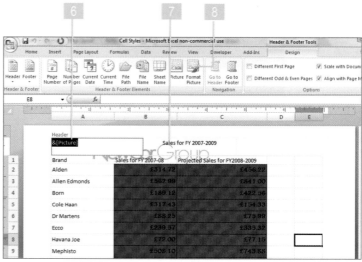

9 Click in a cell to view the logo in its new format.

10 Click the right-hand box and add your name, the date, or another bit of information you want in the header.

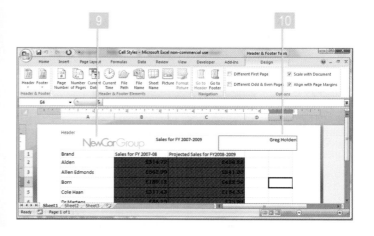

Excel 2007 comes with a set of standard templates you can use to format worksheets. If you create your own custom template, however, you might save some time, especially if you create the same sort of worksheets regularly; you can create a custom template and apply it each time you need to enter new data. Templates can be identified by the filename extension .xltx. Begin by creating a workbook and entering any formatting, formulas or graphics you want the template to contain.

Making a custom template

12

Click the **Office** button.

Point to Save As.

Choose Other Formats.

Choose one of the three formats from the Save as type drop-down list:

■ Excel Template creates an Excel 2007 format template.

■ Excel Macro-Enabled Template. Use this for Excel 2007 templates that use macros.

■ Excel 97-2003. Use this if you want the template to be compatible with earlier versions of Excel.

Type a name for the template.

Click **Save**.

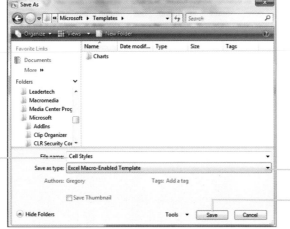

Making a custom template (cont.)

Did you know?

Any custom templates you create can be stored in the Templates folder. That way, Excel can find them easily. The Templates folder is located in \Users\[*current username*]\AppData\Roaming\Microsoft by default (unless you installed Excel in another location). This is not to be confused with the Program Files\Microsoft Office\Templates folder.

There's no reason why your Excel 2007 worksheets need to be dull, grey and boring affairs. In fact, there are three reasons why they should be pleasant to look at. First, Excel gives you the standard Microsoft colour pickers to choose colours. Second, Excel lets you choose colours that are part of themes. Finally, you can choose your own custom colours. You might want to do this if your organisation uses special colours for its printed material and wants your reports to comply with the official look and feel.

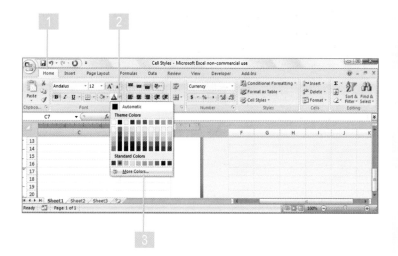

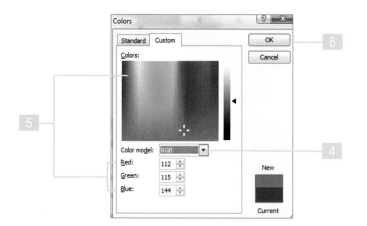

Adding custom colours to a worksheet

1 Click the **Home** tab.

2 Click the **down arrow** next to Font Colour.

3 Choose More Colours....

4 Choose a colour mode (Red-Green-Blue or RGB, or Hue-Saturation-Luminescence or HSL).

5 Enter the colour values, or click the colour you want in the palette.

6 Click **OK**.

The new colour is added to the text you have selected, and is available in the Recent Colours dialogue box.

Adding a scroll bar to a worksheet

Sometimes, the charts you create with Excel end up having so much data to depict that they are wider than the available width of the worksheet. If that's the case, either you need to resize the chart horizontally so it is visible in its entirety, or you can add a scroll bar. The scroll bar is a good option because it doesn't distort the chart, and it gives viewers control over what they want to see.

1 Convert your data to a table. An example of a PivotChart and PivotTable is shown here.

2 Insert two values in the worksheet:

- The initial value of the cell you will link to the scroll bar. Start off with a value of 1.

- The number of values you want to show in the chart. If you want to show 12 months of data, for instance, you want Excel to be able to display up to 12 values, so set this value at 12.

3 Click the **Developer** tab.

4 Click **Insert**.

5 Double-click the **Scroll Bar control** in the Form Controls gallery.

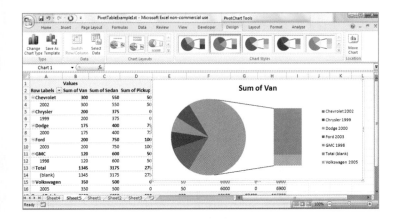

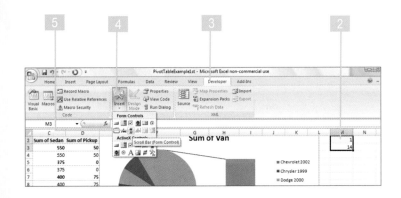

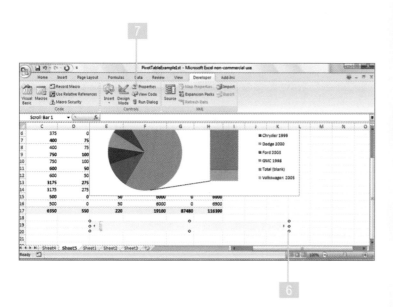

6 When the scroll bar appears, drag the corners to make it the shape you want.

7 Click **Properties**.

8 When the Format Control dialogue box appears, enter the following values:

- Current value: Change this to 1.

- Minimum value. Enter 1.

- Maximum value. Change this to the number of records you want to present in your chart.

- Incremental Change. Set this to 1.

- Page Change. This should be set to the number of data points that you want Excel to scroll through when a viewer clicks. If you have 12 data points (for 12 months), set it to 12, for instance.

- Cell Link. Click inside the range box and then click the cell that you set up to hold the current value of the scroll bar.

9 Click **OK**.

Boosting performance

Introduction

Excel® 2007 gives you an unprecedented capacity to store and manipulate data. But the fact that a worksheet can contain a million rows and 16,000 columns doesn't always translate to an increase in performance. When workbooks and worksheets grow large and complex, it can take a long time to work with them. Simply opening and closing them can be a time-consuming process.

The bigger and more complex the worksheet, the greater your potential for slow calculations. Slow calculations increase your chance of making mistakes. Excel 2007 includes a number of features that are designed to speed up calculations. The most important thing, however, is to configure your worksheet in a way that maximises calculation speed. This chapter's tasks will help you take full advantage of Excel 2007's features and boost performance when you're making calculations.

Performance issues and improvements (in Excel 2007)

The longer you have to tap your fingers and wait for a program to perform a function, the greater your chances that your attention will wander and you'll end up making a mistake. Of course, the faster the processor in your computer and the more memory your computer has, the faster Excel or any other application will work. But there are also ways to optimise the design of your workbooks so calculations are performed more quickly. First, it's important to know something about how Excel 2007 performs calculations.

Excel 2007 has established a wide variety of improvements to the way calculations are performed. For instance:

(a) Excel has increased the memory allocation for formulas and pivot caches to 2GB from 1 GB in Excel 2003.

(b) Smart recalculations are limited only by the memory made available to the program; earlier versions were limited by dependencies.

(c) Sorting levels have been increased to 64; PivotTables can have a maximum of one million rows displayed in a report.

(d) In order to design worksheets more effectively, it's helpful to understand the methods Excel uses to perform calculations.

Excel has a smart calculation 'engine' that continuously tracks precedents for each formula as well as the dependencies (the cells referenced by the formula) and any changes made since the last calculation. When the next calculation is made, Excel recalculates only cells, formulas, values or names that have changed or that have been marked as needing recalculation, as well as cells dependent on other cells that need recalculation. For this reason, it's often much faster the second time you perform a calculation in a workbook, because Excel stores the most recent calculation process, and only recalculates cells or dependants that have changed.

As you know from browsing the web, temporary files accumulate as your computer stores data so you don't have to access it from a remote location every time. Excel, too, stores temporary files on your computer. If too many temporary files accumulate in your \Windows\Temp directory, your computer can slow down. If you find Excel running too slowly, clean out the temp files to free up memory.

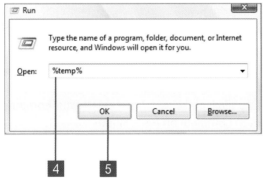

Cleaning out your temporary files

1 Click **Start**.

2 Type Run.

3 When the Run application appears, click it.

4 Type %temp%.

5 Click **OK**.

13

Cleaning out your temporary files (cont.)

6 When the Temp folder opens, click **Views** and choose List.

7 Do one of the following:

- Select any files that pertain to Microsoft Excel, right-click them, and choose Delete.

- Press [Ctrl]+[A] to select all files in the Temp directory, and then press [Del] to delete them.

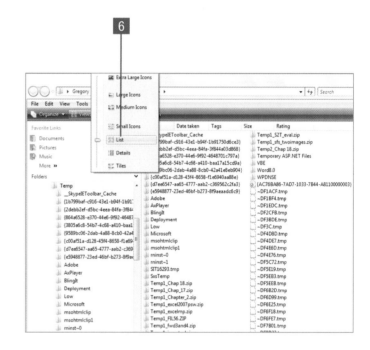

For your information

Installing applications creates temporary files. Often, you are required to restart your computer before you use the applications you have installed. Before you delete temporary files, make sure you restart your computer if required to complete an installation.

Once you delete temporary files or other files to free up memory, you should defragment your computer's hard disk. Defragmentation maximises efficiency and helps your computer find files more quickly because they aren't spread out in separate locations on your hard disk. If your files are contiguous (on adjacent areas of your hard disk), Excel can find data and perform calculations more quickly.

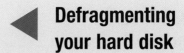

Defragmenting your hard disk

1 Click **Start**.

2 Type Defragmenter.

3 Press [Return] or click **Disk Defragmenter**.

4 When the Disk Defragmenter utility opens, click **Defragment now** to run the program.

13

Did you know?

Windows Vista gives you the ability to schedule regular defragmentations as well, and you can schedule defragmentation sessions to run at times when you're not working (in the middle of the night, for instance).

Exploring Quick Access Toolbar customisation options

1 Locate the Quick Access Toolbar next to the Office button.

2 Pass your pointer over each of the toolbar options to see what's currently there.

Reposition the toolbar

3 Click the **Customise Quick Access Toolbar** button.

4 Choose Show Below the Ribbon. The toolbar moves closer to your work area.

5 Choose Show Above the Ribbon. The toolbar moves back to its original location.

If you haven't used Office 2007 before, it might take some time to familiarise yourself with the ribbon system. Commands that used to be located under familiar menu options in Excel 2003 are located in totally new places and can only be accessed by clicking on the appropriate tabs, each of which has its own ribbon: Home Insert, Page Layout, Formulas, Data, Review, and View. The Quick Access Toolbar, located just above these options, is intended to give you a place to access frequently used options. You can reduce time searching for options and thus speed up your work by customising the ribbon to contain the options you want.

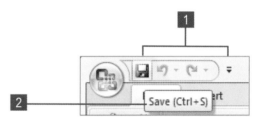

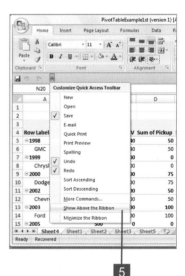

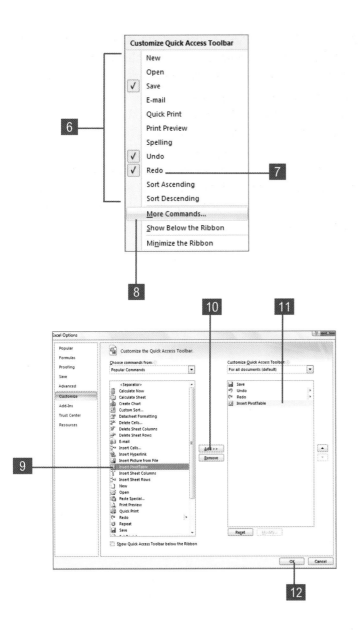

Exploring Quick Access Toolbar customisation options (cont.)

Add a New Toolbar Button

6 Choose any one of the standard options to add it to the Quick Access Toolbar.

7 A check mark indicates that this command is displayed.

8 Choose More Commands ... to add more options to the toolbar.

9 Click one of the available commands on the left side of the Options window.

10 Click **Add**.

11 The option is added to the right side of the window, where visible toolbar options are listed.

12 Click **OK**.

13

Did you know?

The options displayed on the left side of the Options window are only the most popular ones. Click the **down arrow** next to Choose commands from to access a full selection of commands. These include macro commands, Office commands, and many other options.

Controlling calculation options

Excel, like other Office 2007 applications, is configured to perform many tasks automatically by default. This includes calculations. By manually adjusting the way Excel performs calculations, you can speed up the program's operation. This is especially noticeable with large-scale workbooks: if Excel performs calculations automatically every time you make a minute change to the workbook, the program's operation is slowed. You can tell Excel when to perform calculations and work more efficiently.

1 Click the **Formulas** tab.

2 Click **Calculation Options**.

3 Choose one of the popular calculation options:

- Automatic: Every time you make a change, Excel automatically calculates all dependent formulas.

- Automatic except for data tables: Whenever you make a change, Excel automatically calculates all dependent formulas except for those contained in data tables.

- Manual: Excel doesn't do any automatic calculations. It only calculates formulas when you choose Calc Now on the Calculation tab.

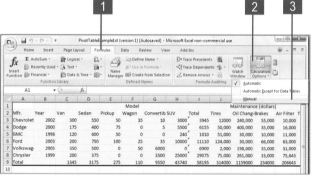

Did you know?

If you choose the manual calculation option, you can quickly tell Excel to recalculate formulas that have altered since the previous calculation was performed. Press [F9] to perform this recalculation for all open workbooks. Similarly, [Shift]+[F9] recalculates only formulas that have changed in the active worksheet. [Ctrl], [Alt]+[F9] recalculates all formulas in all open workbooks whether they have changed or not. [Ctrl], [Shift], [Alt]+[F9] checks dependent formulas and recalculates all formulas in all open workbooks whether they have changed since last time or not.

Iterative calculations are repeated until a specified numeric condition is achieved. If a formula refers back to one of its own cells, it can potentially repeat indefinitely because it is a circular reference. You can limit the maximum number of times a formula will be recalculated to avoid slowdowns. Not only that, but you can also specify the amount of change that a recalculation can produce.

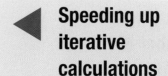

Speeding up iterative calculations

1 Click the **Office** button.

2 Click **Excel Options**.

3 Choose Formulas.

4 Check Enable iterative calculation.

5 Adjust the Maximum Iterations limit as needed.

6 Adjust the Maximum Change from the calculations if needed.

7 Click **OK**.

13

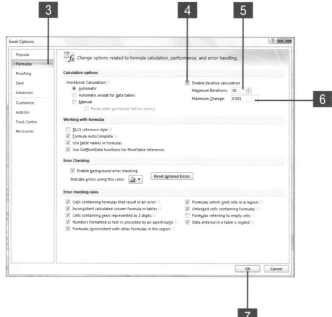

Reducing the number of calculation threads

1 Click the **Office** button.

2 Click **Excel Options**.

3 Click **Advanced**.

4 Scroll down to the Formulas section of the Advanced options.

5 Check the box next to Enable multi-threaded calculation.

6 Choose one of the options for calculation threads:

- Click here to use all available processors your computer has installed.

- Click here to limit the number of processors.

7 Click **OK**.

In previous versions of Excel, advanced options were accessed from the Options dialogue box under the Tools menu. In Excel 2007, you click the **Office** button, choose Excel Options, and click **Advanced**. The advanced options cover many functions of the program, and one is the number of calculation threads you have operating at any one time. A thread is a bit of memory that is allocated for a specific process on a computer. If many threads are being used at once for complex or iterative calculations, Excel can slow down. By limiting the number of threads, you can avoid such slowdowns – or at least limit their effects.

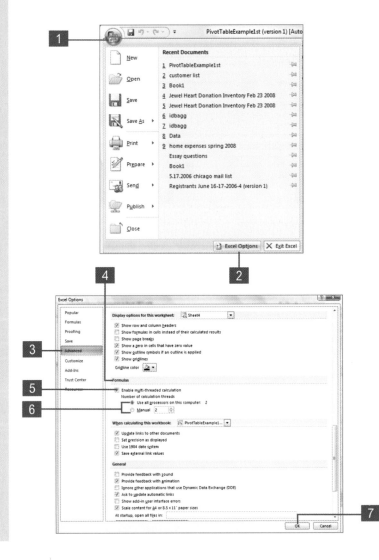

When you first start Excel, if you don't specify calculation options as described in one of the preceding tasks, Excel uses the settings from the first non-add-in workbook you open. You don't have to use this workbook's settings, of course. But you don't have to make a global change that affects all workbooks. You can used the advanced options to make changes that affect only a single worksheet.

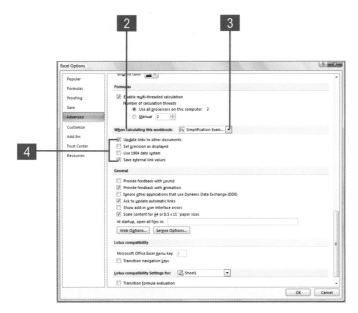

Adjusting calculation options for a single worksheet

1 Follow steps 1 to 3 in the preceding task.

2 Scroll down to the section (below Formulas) called When calculating this workbook:.

3 Choose the open workbook you want to adjust from the drop-down list.

4 Click one or more of the four advanced options:

- Update links to other documents.

- Set precision as displayed. The precision of calculations is set to use stored values by default. Checking this box uses displayed values, not stored ones. For example, if you have set a cell to use a serial number as a stored value in addition to displayed date, the calculation will be performed on the date, not the serial number.

13

Adjusting calculation options for a single worksheet (cont.)

- Use 1904 date system. Dates are critical to interpreting data, and they contribute to how Excel performs calculations. In the 1900 date system, 1 January 1900 is the first date and has a serial value of 1; the last date is 31 December 9999, which has a serial value of 2958465. In the 1904 date system, 2 January 1904 has the serial value of 1 and 31 December 9999 has a serial value of 2957003.

- Save external link values. Click here to save external references to a cell range in another workbook.

5 Click **OK**.

5

Uncovering calculation slowdowns

The sheer size of a workbook isn't the primary reason why calculations can take a long time. Rather, the number of cell references you make to external workbooks and the efficiency of your functions are more important factors.

Reduce repeated calculations and references

Many worksheets are made using formulas that are copied from other worksheets or from one location to another in the same worksheet. Simply deleting unnecessary repeated calculations will speed up processes. Specifically, you need to:

(a) lower the number of references in each formula;

(b) move repeated calculations to helper cells, then reference helper cells from the original formulas;

(c) create new rows or columns to store intermediate calculation results once, as shown opposite.

Make formulas more efficient

Another way to speed up calculation functions is to make your formulas more efficient. This might involve several streamlining approaches:

(a) Reduce the number of cells you reference in SUM and SUMIF functions. Don't include cells you don't need.

(b) Use Excel's built-in functions when possible instead of those written in VBA.

(c) Sort data before you perform lookups on it; lookups on sorted data can be dramatically faster than those on unsorted data.

It's always a good idea to time calculations whenever you make a significant change.

13

Making your formulas simpler

When you have a calculation that involves only a cell or two, Excel will probably perform it in a matter of a few milliseconds. But when you have a workbook that contains thousands of cells and thousands of calculations, it makes a noticeable difference if your formulas are simplified. Here is a simple example of formulas that can be streamlined so they are performed more quickly.

1 Create a worksheet in which column A contains a long series of numbers: type 101 in A1 and 102 in A2.

2 Select both cells.

3 Double-click the **dark square** in the bottom right-hand corner of the bottom cell and drag it down as far as you need.

4 Release the mouse button to add new numbers to the series.

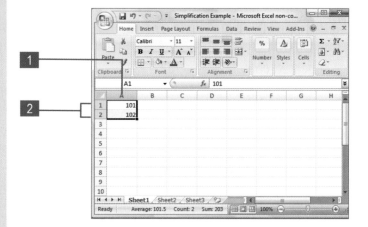

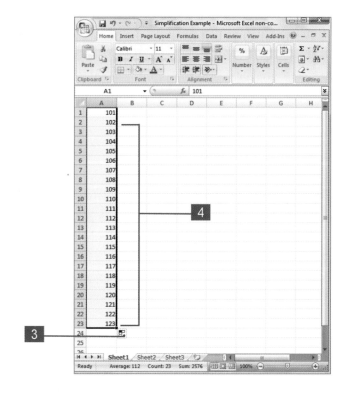

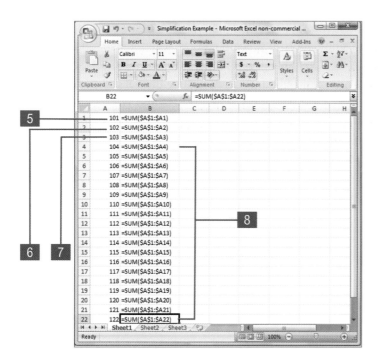

5 Type the formula for the first cell, in cell B1:
=SUM($A$1:$A1).

6 In cell B2, type the formula for the sum of cells A1 and A2:
=SUM($A$1:$A2).

7 In cell B3, type the formula for the sum of cells A1 through A3: =SUM($A$1:$A3).

8 Continue this pattern as far as you can. If you stopped here and had Excel perform all of the calculations in column B, you would be looking at thousands or even millions of sums.

9 By adding a different, and simpler, set of formulas in column C, you greatly reduce the number of calculations Excel has to make.

13

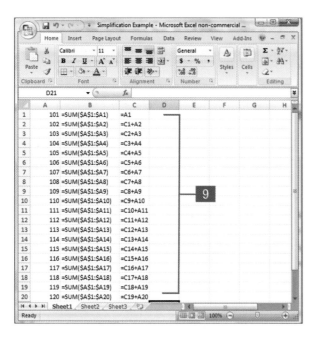

For your information

You have to format the cells as text in order to have the formulas appear rather than numbers. Right-click the cells, choose Format Cells from the context menu, and choose Text.

Exporting data to Microsoft Word

For many Excel users, the ultimate goal of assembling and analysing data is to prepare reports. Often, those reports need to be written in Microsoft Word. How do you export your Excel data into Word? You can simply copy the data by pressing [Ctrl]+[C] in Excel, then paste the data into Word by pressing [Ctrl]+[C]. But if you use the Paste Special command you'll be able to work with the data in Word and make changes to it. Make sure you open both the workbook you want to export and the Word file to which you plan to export it before you follow these steps.

1 Select the cells you want to copy in your Excel workbook.

2 Click the **Home** tab, if necessary.

3 Click **Copy**.

4 Make your Word document the active one.

5 Click the **Home** tab if necessary.

6 Click **Paste** and choose Paste Special.

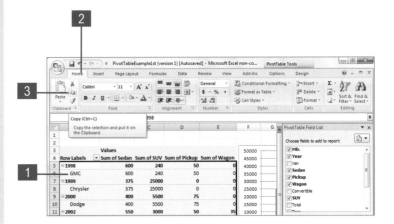

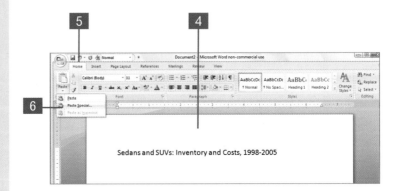

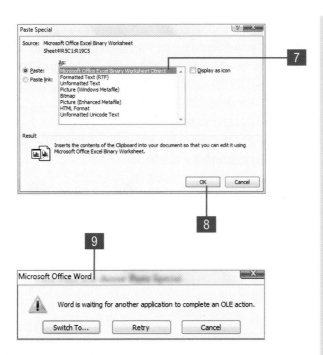

7 Choose Microsoft Office Excel Binary Worksheet Document.

8 Click **OK**.

9 If this dialogue box appears, switch back to your Excel file.

10 Click **Disable Macros** and switch back to the Word file.

11 Click **Retry**.

12 When the data is pasted, click a cell to make sure you can change the data.

13

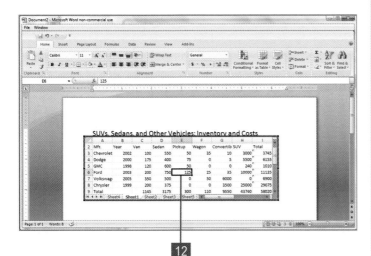

Sharing a workbook

It sometimes happens that two or more workers need to be entering or editing data on the same spreadsheet. One way to do this is for one person to enter the data, save the changes and close the file, and tell the other person to open the file and work on it as needed. But this is time consuming. If you and your co-worker(s) are on a network, you can both open the worksheet at the same time and edit it simultaneously. You can do this by sharing the workbook.

1. Click **Review**.
2. Click **Share Workbook**.
3. Check the box next to 'Allow changes by more than one user at the same time.'
4. Click the **Advanced** tab.

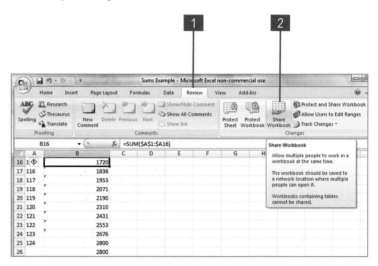

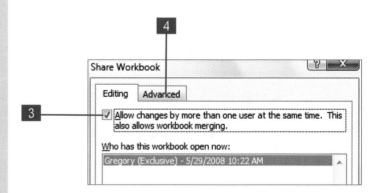

Share Workbook

Editing | Advanced

Track changes
- ◉ Keep change history for: 30 days
- ○ Don't keep change history

Update changes
- ○ When file is saved
- ◉ Automatically every: 15 minutes
  - ◉ Save my changes and see others' changes
  - ○ Just see other users' changes

Conflicting changes between users
- ◉ Ask me which changes win
- ○ The changes being saved win

Include in personal view
- ☑ Print settings
- ☑ Filter settings

OK | Cancel

5 Under Update changes, click the button next to Automatically every:

6 Change the time interval if you wish.

7 Click **OK**.

13

See also

See my book *Brilliant Home* and *Wireless Networks* for tips on setting up a network so you and your co-workers or family members can share files.

Working with Excel 2007 add-ins

Introduction

You would think Excel 2007 has everything you need to use the program, but you would be missing some important additional tools that are available to you. The program can do a lot, but if you want it perform special functions, you add them to the program as add-ins. Add-ins are macros that have been provided by their developers so that you can add them as buttons or menu options in the Excel interface. By choosing the new interface options, you run the add-in (the macro) and perform lookups, conditional sums, or other calculations. This chapter shows you how to install add-ins and use them to work smarter with Excel.

Add-ins and Excel 2007

Some of the add-ins that are available to you are specific to Excel, while others are part of the Office 2007 package. You get a complete list of both kinds of add-ins when you click **Excel**

Options and click **Add-Ins**. The add-ins listed in the middle of the screen (see below) with 'Office 12' as part of their location are available to be used with all Office 2007 applications.

Name	Location	Type	
Active Application Add-ins			
SpBasic Language Add-In	C:\...\spBasic\AddIns\spBasic\SpBasicAddIn.xla	Excel Add-in	
Inactive Application Add-ins			
Analysis ToolPak	analys32.xll	Excel Add-in	
Analysis ToolPak - VBA	atpvbaen.xlam	Excel Add-in	
Conditional Sum Wizard	sumif.xlam	Excel Add-in	
Custom XML Data	C:\...es\Microsoft Office\Office12\OFFRHD.DLL	Document Inspector	
Date (Smart tag lists)	C:\...iles\microsoft shared\Smart Tag\MOFL.DLL	Smart Tag	
Euro Currency Tools	eurotool.xlam	Excel Add-in	≡
Financial Symbol (Smart tag lists)	C:\...iles\microsoft shared\Smart Tag\MOFL.DLL	Smart Tag	
Headers and Footers	C:\...es\Microsoft Office\Office12\OFFRHD.DLL	Document Inspector	
Hidden Rows and Columns	C:\...es\Microsoft Office\Office12\OFFRHD.DLL	Document Inspector	
Hidden Worksheets	C:\...es\Microsoft Office\Office12\OFFRHD.DLL	Document Inspector	
Internet Assistant VBA	C:\...rosoft Office\Office12\Library\HTML.XLAM	Excel Add-in	
Invisible Content	C:\...es\Microsoft Office\Office12\OFFRHD.DLL	Document Inspector	
Lookup Wizard	lookup.xlam	Excel Add-in	
Person Name (Outlook e-mail recipients)	C:\...es\microsoft shared\Smart Tag\FNAME.DLL	Smart Tag	
Solver Add-in	solver.xlam	Excel Add-in	
Document Related Add-ins			
No Document Related Add-ins			▼

The concept of add-ins that are provided with a program so you don't have to install them seems like an oxymoron. Add-ins are supposed to be 'extras', aren't they? Nevertheless, you might already have some add-ins available without having to 'add' them. For instance, if you click the Formulas tab and see a Solutions group with Conditional Sums and Lookup buttons above it, that means you have the Formulas and Conditional Sums add-ins already installed. If you don't see these two options, adding the add-ins that come with Excel 2007 is an easy matter, however.

Implementing Excel's built-in add-ins

1 Click the **Office** button.

2 Click **Excel Options**.

3 Click **Add-Ins**.

4 Make sure Excel Add-Ins is displayed.

5 Click **Go**.

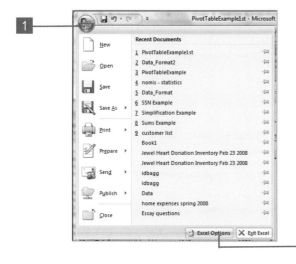

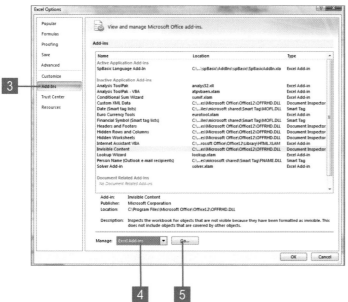

14

Implementing Excel's built-in add-ins (cont.)

6 Check the boxes next to the add-ins you want to install.

7 Click **OK**.

8 If you see this dialogue box, click **Yes**. (You might have to repeat this step more than once, depending on which add-ins you want to install.)

9 When a User Account Control dialogue appears, click **OK**.

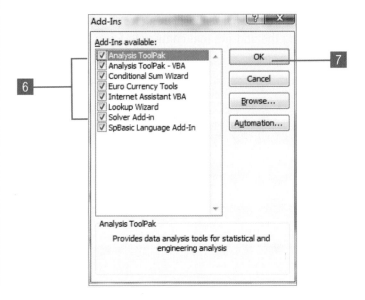

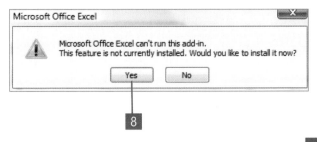

The Solver add-in can be used when you need to predict how results can change over time as assumptions change. Suppose you expect to sell a specific quota of shoes each month for the next three months. You can use the Solver to take into account the expectations and sales quotas for each month and adjust sales quotas to meet the goal.

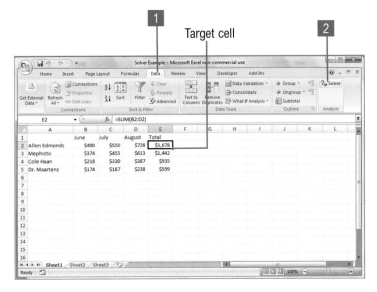

Target cell

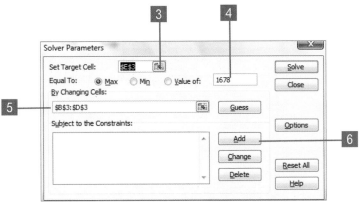

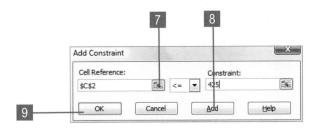

1 Click the **Data** tab.

2 Click the **Solver** button in the Solutions group.

3 Select the Target cell.

4 Specify the Equal to option and enter a value if necessary.

5 Specify the range of cells you want Solver to compare against the target cell.

6 Click **Add**.

7 Enter specific cell references and constraints.

8 Click **Add**. You may want to select a cell in a particular row and add a sales figure that is less than the desired quota, for instance. You can add multiple cell constraints.

9 Click **OK** to close Add Constraints.

14

Loading the
Solver (cont.)

[10] Click **Solve**.

[11] When Solver finds a solution, the Solver Results dialogue box will appear.

[12] Click a report type.

[13] Click **OK**.

[14] Click the Answer Report tab to view the report.

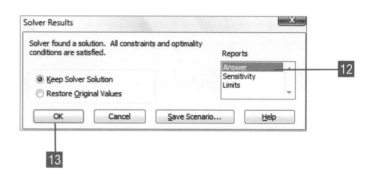

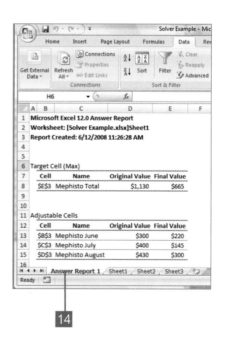

The Conditional Sum wizard add-in leads you step-by-step through the process of creating formulas that use the SUM and IF functions, and that are often confusing to create manually. The IF function is a logical function: one that is used to test for a specific condition. It applies conditional tests to data and returns values based on the arguments logical_test, value_if_true, and value_if_false. The wizard makes building a conditional formula doable if not downright easy.

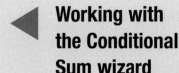
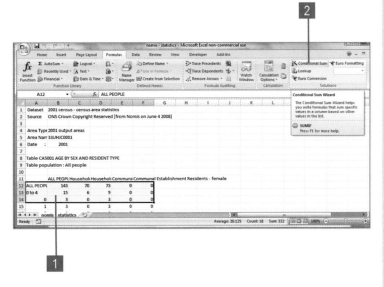

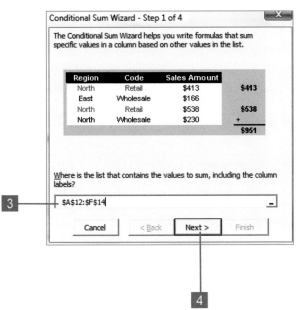

1 Select the table that contains the data you want to use – or the cells within the table on which you want to apply the formula.

2 Click the **Conditional Sum** button on the Formulas tab to display the first screen of the wizard.

3 Select the range you want to use, or use the range represented by the data you selected in step 1.

4 Click **Next**.

14

Working with the Conditional Sum wizard (cont.)

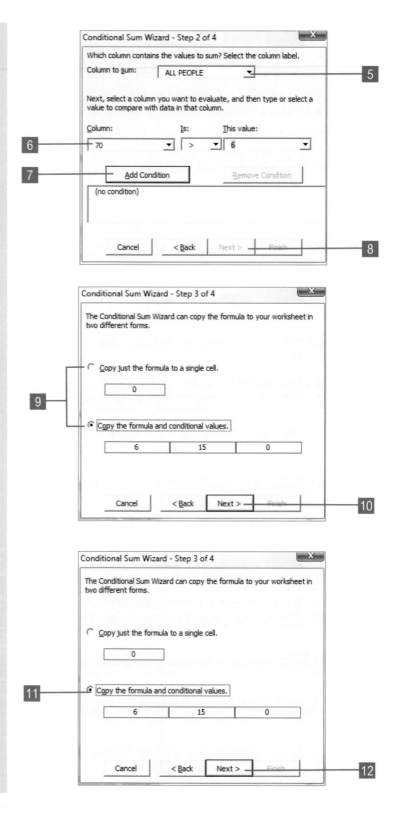

5 In the second screen, click the **Column To Sum** drop-down list and choose the name of the column from which you want to calculate a sum.

6 Specify contains to use when selecting the values you want in the sum.

7 Click **Add Condition**.

8 Click **Next**.

9 In the third screen, choose one of two options:

- Copy just the formula to a single cell.

- Copy the formula and conditional values.

10 Click **Next**.

11 Click one of the cells in the table where you want to locate the formula and its location is added to the fourth screen.

12 Click **Next**.

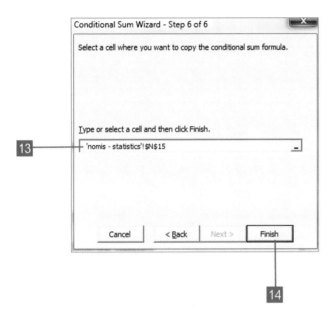

Conditional Sum Wizard - Step 6 of 6

Select a cell where you want to copy the conditional sum formula.

Type or select a cell and then click Finish.

'nomis - statistics'!$N$15

Cancel   < Back   Next >   Finish

12 Click one of the cells in the table where you want to locate the result, and its location is added to the last screen.

13 Click **Finish**.

For your information

Don't use blank space characters when typing cell locations or other data in the Conditional Sum wizard. The wizard will simply ignore it. If the space is part of the string you are using to construct your formula, the results might be incorrect.

Using the Lookup Wizard

The Lookup Wizard add-in creates formulas by using the INDEX and MATCH functions, and streamlines the process of creating lookup formulas. In contrast to the Lookup function that's built into Excel, the wizard helps you look up information step by step.

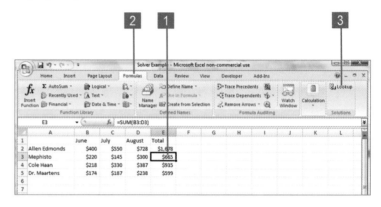

1 Select the table that contains the data you want to use in creating your formula.

2 Click the **Formulas** tab.

3 Click the **Lookup** button.

4 If the first screen doesn't contain the range of cells you want to work with, drag in the table itself to add the correct cells.

5 Click **Next**.

6 Specify the column and row that contains the data you want to locate.

7 Click **Next**.

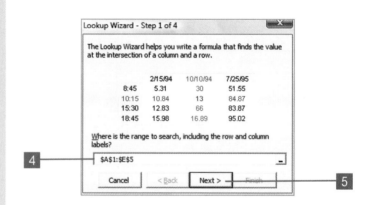

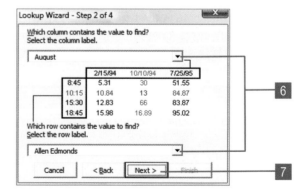

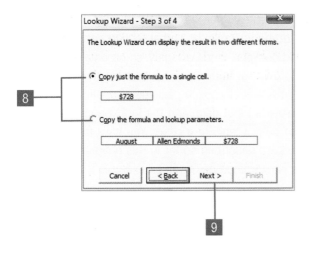

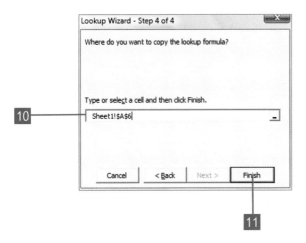

8 Decide whether you want the lookup values to be included in your worksheet (by choosing Copy the formula and lookup parameters) or by choosing Copy just the formula to a single cell.

9 Click **Next**.

10 Choose the cell where you want the formula to be located. (Click directly in the table to select the cell.)

11 Click **Finish**.

The formula is added to the formula box, and the result is inserted in the cell you specified earlier.

14

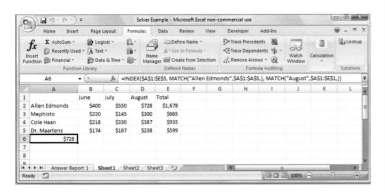

Performing 'what if?' analyses

The add-in called the Analysis ToolPak is a set of tools (described briefly in Table 14.1) that let you perform many different and complex kinds of analyses on data. Each of the tools has its own variations on how data is processed, so this single add-in is actually a rich package of applications. In each case, you provide input data, and the tool you choose shows results in an output table or a chart. You have to load this add-in like the others described so far in this chapter. One of the many tools is examined below as an example.

Generating random numbers

1. Click **Data**.

2. Click **Data Analysis**.

3. Click **Random Number Generation**.

4. Click **OK**.

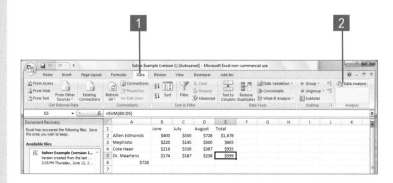

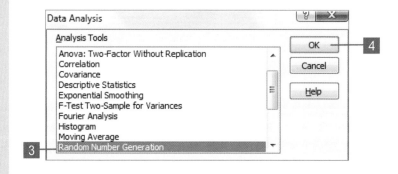

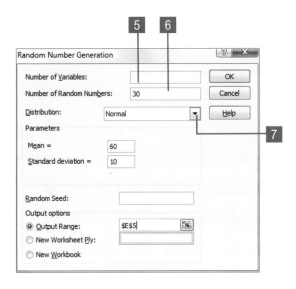

Performing 'what if?' analyses (cont.)

5 Enter a number here only if you want to generate more than one set of random numbers. Otherwise, leave the box blank, in which case Excel will use the number of columns specified in Output Range.

6 Enter how many random numbers you want to generate.

7 Check the type of distribution you want to use. Options are:

- Uniform: Generates numbers with equal probablility.

- Normal: Produces numbers in a bell curve distribution.

- Binomial: Generates random numbers characterised by the probability of success over a number of trials.

- Bernoulli: Generates a random series of 1s and 0s based on the probability of success in a single trial.

- Poisson: Generates random numbers based on the probability of a designated number of events occurring in a time frame.

14

Working with Excel 2007 add-ins 261

Performing 'what if?' analyses (cont.)

- ■ Patterned: Generates random numbers according to a pattern characterised by a lower and upper bound, a step value, and a repetition rate.

- ■ Discrete: Generates random numbers from a series of values and probabilities for those values (in which the sum of the probabilities equals 1).

8 Enter the parameters for the selected distribution.

9 Enter a Random Seed number Excel should use to generate the random numbers. If you leave the box blank, Excel will generate a different set each time.

10 Select a location for the output.

11 Click **OK**. Excel calculates a set of random numbers and displays them in the worksheet.

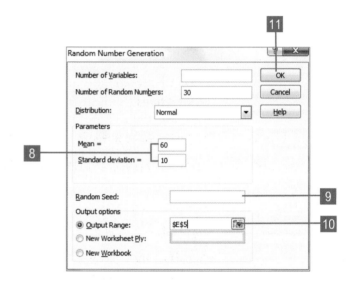

Table 14.1 Analysis ToolPak Tools

Tool	What it does
Anova: Single Factor	Performs basic analysis of data variance on two or more samples.
Anova: Two-Factor With Replication	Performs analysis of data in two different dimensions at the same time.
Anova: Two-Factor Without Replication	Performs analysis in two different dimensions, but there is only a single observation for each pair.
Correlation	Calculates the correlation coefficient between two variables for a number of subjects. It outputs a correlation matrix that shows how the two variables move and 'vary together'.
Covariance	Similar to the Correlation tool in that it also shows the correlation coefficient between each pair of measurement variables. Use it to show whether or not two variables tend to move together, not how they move together.
Descriptive Statistics	Analyses the central tendency and variability of your data by generating a report showing statistics for your input data.
Exponential Smoothing	Predicts a value in the future based on a forecast for a prior period.
F-Test Two-Sample for Variances	Compares variances among two populations (for example, two sports teams, two political parties) by performing a two-sample F-test – in other words, it calculates the value *f* of an F-statistic.
Fourier Analysis	Uses the Fast Fourier Transform (FFT) method to transform data and analyse periodic data.
Histogram	Generates data for the number of times a value occurs within a set of data. Results are presented in an easy-to-read histogram table.

14

Performing 'what if?' analyses (cont.)

Moving Average	An excellent tool for predicting sales or future trends. It predicts values in a future period, based on the average value of that same value over a previous period.
Random Number Generation	Fills a range with independent random numbers you can use to characterise a population.
Rank and Percentile	Contains the ordinal and percentage rank of each value in a data set so you can analyse the relative standing of values in the set.
Regression	Uses the 'least squares' method to perform linear regression analysis – it fits a line through a set of variables.
Sampling	If you have a population that is too large to process, create a sample from it using this tool.
t-Test	Computes a t-statistic value that tests for the equality of the population means underlying each sample.
z-Test	Can be used to test the null hypothesis that there is no difference between two population means.

Installing more Excel 2007 add-ins

The add-ins that come with Excel 2007 are the ones you are most likely to use. But you should know about a few other add-ins that Microsoft and others have made for the application. They need to be downloaded and installed before you can use them. But they can help you save time performing a few specialised tasks.

When you download an add-in, you need to know where it is installed. Usually, when you download the file, you are given two choices: you can click **Save** to save the files to your computer, or **Run** to open and install them automatically. For instance, when you download the Synchronising Tables with SharePoint Lists add-in, you can save it to your desktop. Double-click the file to install it. When the prompt appears, make a note of where the files will be saved. On my system, they were installed by default in C:\ 2007 Office System Developer Resources\Code Samples. (You can click **Browse** and install in another location.)

Once you know where the add-in is located, switch to Excel and follow these steps:

1. Click the **Office** button.

2. Click **Excel Options**.

3. Click **Add-Ins**.

4. Click **Go** next to Manage Excel Add-Ins.

5. When the Add-Ins dialogue box opens, click **Browse**. Navigate to the add-in you installed earlier. Double-click the file. It is added to the list of available Excel add-ins, as shown below. (It is called Synchronisewssandexcel.)

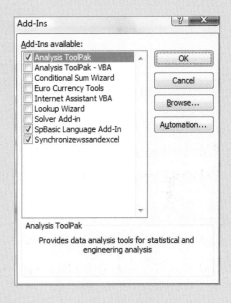

6. Click **OK**.

You can then access the add-in from one of Excel's ribbons. It might be the Data or the Formula ribbon. However, the SharePoint add-in described above is harder to find. You have to have a table open; you find it in the form of a Publish and allow Sync button added to Table Tools.

Synchronising tables

In Chapter 10, you learnt how Excel can interact with lists that are part of an online sharing environment called SharePoint. Excel 2003 had the ability to communicate with SharePoint data built into it; Excel 2007 does not. However, Microsoft, on its Office website, includes an add-in for Excel 2007 designed to synchronise data contained in an Excel table with a list published in a SharePoint site. You'll find the add-in at **http://www.microsoft.com/downloads/details.aspx? familyid=25836e52-1892-4e17-ac08-5df13cfc5295**. After you download and install the add-in, follow these steps.

1. Open the table you want to synchronise with the SharePoint site.

2. Click anywhere in the table to activate the Table Tools ribbon.

3. Click **Publish and allow Sync**.

4. Type the URL of the SharePoint site where you want to publish the table.

5. Type your name.

6. Type a description of the file.

7. Click **Publish**.

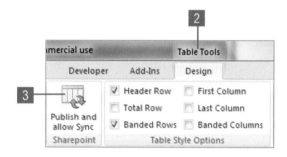

For your information

You need to save your worksheet in Excel 97-2003 file format before you can publish it using the add-in.

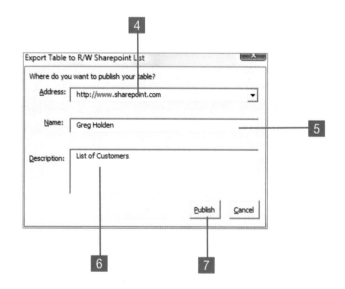

Another add-in makes it possible for you to use a web page as a data source in Excel. You find it at the Microsoft Research site: go to **http://research.microsoft.com/research/downloads** and search for Excel 2007 Web Data Add-In. Click **Download**, and install the program. Close and then restart Excel to start using the add-in.

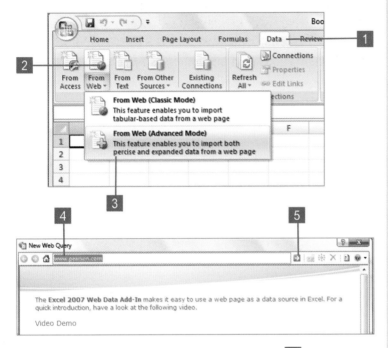

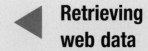

1 Click **Data**.

2 Click **From Web**. The drop-down option From Web (Advanced Mode) is the option provided by the add-in.

3 Choose From Web (Advanced Mode).

4 Type the URL of the web page you want to access.

5 Click the green **Next** button.

6 Click **Capture Data**.

7 Double-click an object on the web page to add it to the spreadsheet below.

14

Macros, shortcuts and other timesavers

Introduction

Once you've acquainted yourself with Excel 2007's many basic features, you'll naturally appreciate going a step or two beyond the basics to learn some shortcuts and timesavers. In this chapter, you'll learn ways to automate procedures you carry out frequently with Excel. You'll also get a rundown of common keyboard shortcuts and other shortcuts that will help you to keep your productivity level high while maximising your valuable time as well.

15

Pros and cons of working with macros

The fact that this book consists of step-by-step instructions reflects the way you work with Microsoft Excel itself: you move through a series of steps in order to perform a task. For instance, with a simple sum: you open a workbook, click the sheet you want, select the cells that contain the data you want to add, and click the **Sum** button on the Home tab. If you need to add up many series of cells, you repeatedly follow the same series of steps, which quickly becomes monotonous. To avoid such tiresome repetition, you can create a small-scale application called a macro that runs through the steps with a single command.

One of the nice things about macros is that you don't need to be a programmer to create them. You record the steps you want the macro to contain, using a built-in Excel command. Excel stores the command with a name of your choice. You store the macro either in the workbook you're working on presently, in a new workbook, or in the Personal Macro workbook, where you can access it from any file you're using. Once you create the macro, you can edit it or add comments to it so your colleagues can understand what it does and decide if they want to use it themselves.

The potential downside of macros is the fact that, when you try to use a macro someone else has

created, you don't know with total certainty what kinds of commands are contained in it. Macros can contain viruses and other malicious code that can harm your files. But Excel, in the Security command of Excel Options, includes some safety features that make it impossible for macros to operate without your approval.

To run a macro, you click the **Macro** command on either the View or Developer tab. Or you can use a shortcut key that you have assigned to it. You can also assign a Quick Access Toolbar button to it. The Macro dialogue box, which opens when you click the **Macro** button, lets you run, edit, test, or delete Excel macros you already have, or create a new one.

Keyboard Shortcuts in Excel 2007

Keyboard shortcuts are important timesavers for many repetitive functions in Excel 2007, including macros. You are given the opportunity to assign a sequence of keys to a macro just before you record one. In addition, Excel has a variety of

keyboard shortcuts for many common commands. Some of the more popular ones are listed below. Many more keyboard shortcuts are available; search Help for 'Excel shortcut and function keys' and you'll find more.

Shortcut	What it does
Navigate a worksheet	
Arrow keys	Move up, down, left, or right one cell at a time
[Home]	Jump to beginning of row
[Ctrl]+[Home]	Jump to beginning of worksheet
[Ctrl]+[End]	Jump to bottom right corner of worksheet
[Page Down]	Move down one screen
[Page Up]	Move up one screen
[Alt]+[Page Down]	Move one screen to the right
[Alt]+[Page Up]	Move one screen to the left
[F5] or [Ctrl]+[G]	Opens the Go To dialogue box
[Ctrl]+[Page Up]	Move to previous worksheet
[Ctrl]+[Page Down]	Move to next worksheet
Select data	
[Ctrl]+[*]	Selects every cell adjacent to the current cell
[Shift]+navigation	Moves the active cell in the direction of the navigation key (see Navigate a worksheet, above)

Shortcut	What it does
[Ctrl]+[Spacebar]	Selects the entire column (or columns) that contains the active cell (or cells)
[Shift]+[Spacebar]	Selects entire row (or rows) that contains the active cell (or cells)
[F8]	Toggles (turns on and off) the ability to extend the current selection using navigation keys
[Ctrl]+[Shift + O]	Selects all cells in current worksheet that contain comments
Edit a worksheet	
[F2]	Lets you edit the active cell
[Shift]+[F2]	Lets you insert or edit a comment in the active cell
[Alt]+[=]	Lets you enter an AutoSum formula into the current cell
[Alt]+[Enter]	Insert line break in a cell that has wrapped text
[Ctrl]+[Enter]	Fills selected cells with contents of the Formula Bar

15

Recording a macro

Consider creating a macro whenever you find yourself performing the same series of steps over and over again, or if you need to add new functions to Excel. You have two options for creating a macro: you can record one by performing the set of steps and saving them with a keyboard shortcut, or you can write one using the Visual Basic for Applications (VBA) programming language. Recording is described in this task, VBA in the task that follows. In either case, the macros you create for a workbook are a series of Visual Basic codes, and are stored in the form of a macro module.

1 When you are ready to perform the steps that you want the macro to contain, click the **View** or **Developer** tab.
If you click the Developer tab, you only need to click **Record Macro**. The View tab is shown here.

2 Click **Macros**.

3 Choose **Record Macro** from the drop-down list.

4 Type a name for your macro.

5 Assign a keyboard shortcut to your macro.

6 Decide where to store the macro: in the current workbook, a new workbook, or your Personal Macro workbook.

7 Type a brief but clear description of what the macro does so you and your co-workers know what will happen if they choose it.

8 Click **OK**.

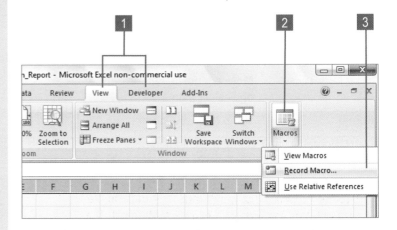

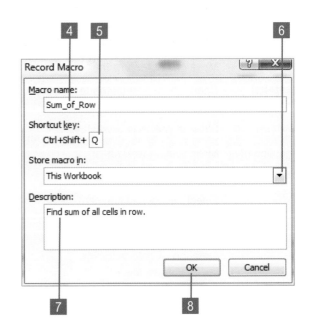

10

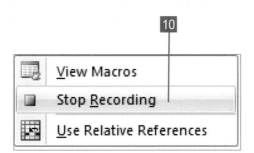

	View Macros
	Stop Recording
	Use Relative References

9 Perform the steps that you want the macro to contain.

10 Click **View** and choose Stop Recording.

For your information

When you name a macro, the name must begin with a character or underscore, and must not include blank spaces. When you assign a keyboard shortcut to a macro, try to pick a shortcut that does not interfere with a built-in keyboard function (such as [Ctrl]+[S] for saving a file). If you type a name that conflicts with a built-in macro or a shortcut that conflicts with another, a dialogue box will appear that alerts you to the problem, so you can make another choice.

15

Creating a macro using Visual Basic

When you create a macro with VBA, you gain more control over the contents: you create the contents of the macro step by step. This option is more complicated than recording a macro. But familiarising yourself with VBA has other benefits. You can debug macros that aren't working correctly, and you can control the way macros play. It's good to at least know about this option even if you don't plan on doing large-scale programming with VBA.

1 Click the **Developer** or **View** tab. (In this example, the Developer tab is shown.)

2 Click **Macros**.

3 Type a name for the macro.

4 Click the **down arrow** next to Macros in, and choose to save the macro in All Open Workbooks or pick a workbook in which you want to store it.

5 Click **Create**.

The Microsoft Visual Basic window opens.

6 In the Module window, type new Visual Basic commands between the **Sub** and **End Sub** lines (or edit existing lines of code).

7 If necessary, press [F2] or Choose Object Browser from the file menu to display the Object Browser, which can help you insert commands.

8 To run the macro, press [F5].

9 Click the **Save** button to save your work. Then click the **File** menu and choose Close and Return to Microsoft Excel.

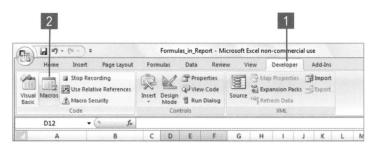

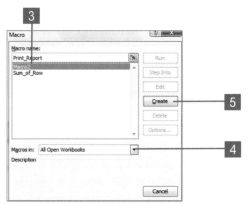

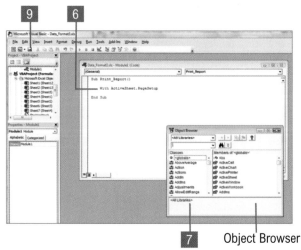

Object Browser

Once you create a macro, the place where you save it becomes important. You might save it in one particular workbook, but that means it's not automatically available to another one. You can, however, copy a macro module from one workbook to another.

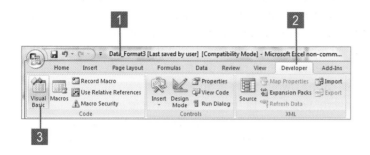

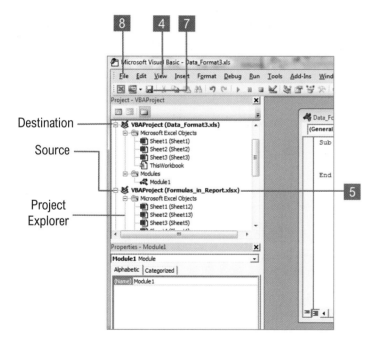

Destination

Source

Project Explorer

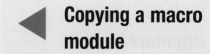

Copying a macro module

1. Open the workbook that contains the macro module you want to copy.

2. Click the **Developer** tab.

3. Click the **Visual Basic** button.

4. Click the **View** menu.

5. Click **Project Explorer**.

6. Drag the module you want to copy from the source workbook to the destination workbook.

7. Click the **Save** button.

8. Click **File** and choose Close and Return to Microsoft Excel.

15

Adding a digital signature to a macro

A digital signature is a complex code generated by a formula called an algorithm. Attaching a digital signature to a file helps certify that you are the owner of the file and no attempt has been made to send the file fraudulently. If Excel detects a problem with a macro (such as potentially malicious code) and the file has been digitally signed, the macro is automatically disabled. In addition, the message bar appears with a note telling you of the problem. You can then click **Options** in the message bar to find out more about the problem. You can then contact the owner to fix it. To add your own digital signature to a macro, you need to use the Visual Basic editor.

1 Open the workbook that contains the macro you want to sign.

2 Click the **Developer** tab.

3 Click the **Visual Basic** button.

4 Click the **Tools** menu.

5 Choose Digital Signature....

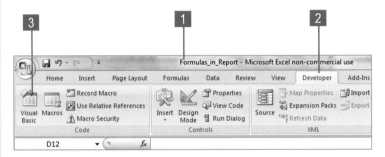

6 Click **Choose**.

7 Choose a certificate.

8 Click here if you want to learn more about the certificate.

9 Click **OK**.

10 Click **OK** to close the Digital Signature dialogue box.

11 Click **Save**.

12 Click **File** and then choose Close and Return to Microsoft Excel.

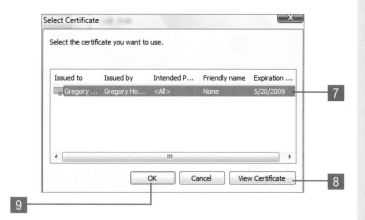

For your information

One of the problems with macros is that they can contain malicious code. Someone may be trying to send you the macro fraudulently in order to inject a virus into your file system. If a digital signature has potential problems, you can click **Show Signature Details** to view details. A problem with the signature will be indicated by a red X.

15

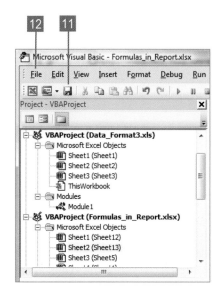

Running and stopping your stored macros

Once you have created macros or copied the ones you need so they can be accessed by the workbook on which you are currently working, it's an easy matter to run or stop them. You have several options for running macros. Once you run them, you can also edit and manage them, as you'll see in subsequent tasks.

Run a macro

1 Do one of the following:

- Press the keyboard shortcut for the macro if you know it.

- Click the **Macros** button on the View or the Developer tab and click **Macros**.

- If you are in the Visual Basic window, click **Edit**, and then press [F5].

2 If you click the **Macros** button, select the macro you want from the list.

3 Click **Run** or press [Ctrl]+[F8].

Stop a macro

4 Do one of the following to stop a macro before it completes executing:

- Press the [Esc] key to stop the macro while it is running.

- Press [Ctrl]+[Break].

Did you know?

Shortcut keys in Excel, for macros and other functions, are case-sensitive. You can create shortcut keys for both [Ctrl]+[F] and [Ctrl]+[f]. If a shortcut key is already used for [Ctrl]+[F], for instance, you can assign [Ctrl]+[f] to a macro instead.

Excel gives you a good deal of control over editing, stopping, and otherwise managing macros, both through the Macro window in Excel itself and through the Visual Basic application. Some of the more common ways to manage macros are described in this section.

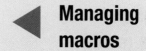

Managing macros

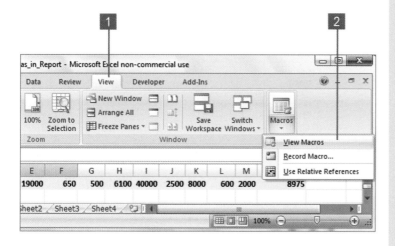

Deleting a macro

1 Click the **Developer** or **View** tab.

2 Click the **Macros** button (if you used the Developer tab). Click **View Macros** on the View tab, as shown here.

3 Click the macro you want to delete.

4 Click **Delete**. Click **Delete** a second time to confirm.

Editing a macro

5 Click the **Developer** tab (shown here), or the **View** tab.

6 Click **Macros**.

15

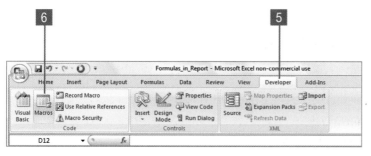

Managing
macros (cont.)

7 Select the macro you want to edit.

8 Click **Edit**.

9 Click the Module window that contains the Visual Basic code for your macro.

10 Type new commands or edit existing ones.

11 Click **Save**.

12 Click **File** and choose Close and Return to Microsoft Excel.

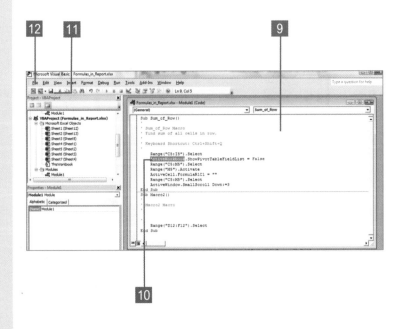

As you learned in Chapter 6, functions can be used as part of formulas in Excel to build calculated fields, perform iterations, or handle other texts. You can type a function into a formula either by manually typing it, or by using the Insert Function dialogue box.

Type the function

To add a VBA function into a formula manually, follow this format:

```
WorkbookName.xls|FunctionName (arguments)
```

Here, *WorkbookName* is the name of the workbook that contains the function. *FunctionName* is the name of the function, and *arguments* is the list of values for the function's arguments.

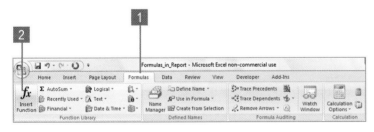

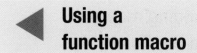
Use the Insert Function method

1 Click the **Formulas** tab.

2 Click **Insert Function**.

3 In the Insert Function dialogue box, choose All from the Or select a category list to make sure all VBA functions are listed.

4 Choose the function you want.

5 Click **OK**.

15

Adding macros to the Quick Access Toolbar

It can be hard to remember all the keyboard shortcuts for your macros, especially if you create quite a few of them. Another way to start a macro quickly is to add it to the Quick Access Toolbar, which is always available near the top of the Excel window. When you mouse over a macro button you've added to the Quick Access Toolbar, a ScreenTip appears to tell you the macro's name and the name of the workbook in which it is contained.

1. Click the **down arrow** on the right edge of the toolbar.

2. Choose More Commands...

3. When the Customise the Quick Access Toolbar window opens, under the Choose command from: drop-down list, choose Macros.

4. Make sure For all documents (default) appears under Customise Quick Access Toolbar.

5. In the left column, click the macro you want to add to the toolbar.

6. Click **Add**.

7. Click the **Move Up** or **Move Down** buttons to arrange the toolbar commands in the order you want.

8. Leave the macro selected in the right column, and click **Modify**.

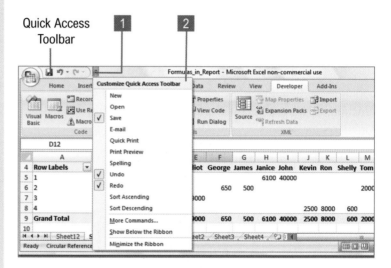

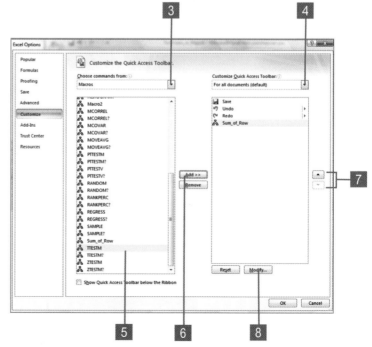

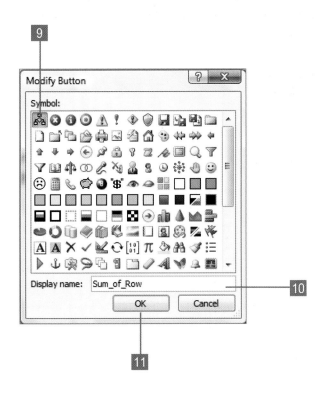

9 Choose an icon to represent the macro on the Quick Access Toolbar.

10 Type a name for the macro.

11 Click **OK**.

12 Click **OK** to close the Customise the Quick Access Toolbar window.

15

Jargon buster

AutoComplete – An Excel 2007 feature that automatically completes your entries based on labels you typed previously.

AutoFill – Excel's ability to automatically fill in adjacent cells with data using the fill handle.

Cell Address – The intersection of a column and row that is applied to a cell.

Command Buttons – Buttons or other controls in the Ribbon that let you perform functions on an Excel document.

Conditional Formatting – Formatting that lets the value of a cell determine how it is formatted.

Fill Handle – A black triangle in the bottom right-hand corner of a cell that automatically fills in data based on the data in adjacent cells.

Formula – An operator and cell range that calculates values in order to arrive at a result.

Function – The combination of an operator and cell range that performs predefined calculations.

Label – Text within a cell that identifies its contents so readers can interpret the contents more easily.

Nested Function – A function that uses another function as one of its arguments.

Office Button – The button at the top left-hand corner of Excel or other Office 2007 applications; it takes the place of the previous File menu.

Quick Access Toolbar – A control near the top of the Excel window that contains shortcuts to frequently used functions and that can be customised freely.

Range – A group of cells that has been selected; the cells can be either contiguous or discontiguous.

Ribbon – A feature new to Excel 2007; a set of tabs and controls at the top of the Excel menu.

SharePoint – A environment that enables collaborators to access shared documents, create new files, and collaborate via a centralised, web-based set of resources.

Smart Tag – A way of labelling data that lets you integrate actions normally performed in other programs directly in Excel.

Task Pane – A window within the main window that opens when you need it or when you click a Dialog Box Launcher icon.

Template – A predesigned layout and set of formatting instructions (fonts, colours, etc.) that you can apply to a workbook quickly so you don't have to apply the formatting from scratch.

Theme – A set of unified design elements that gives a workbook a consistent style.

Value – A number entered in a cell.

Workbook – A basic Excel file, which contains one or more subunits called worksheets.

Worksheet – A single page within a workbook. Each worksheet can have its own formatting.

.xls – The Excel 97-2003 basic workbook format.

.xlsx – A format new to Excel 2007, the basic Excel Workbook format.

XML – Extensible Markup Language, a data interchange format that reduces file sizes. You can save an Excel file in .xlsx or XML format.

XPS – XPS Document format, a format that preserves Microsoft-based formatting in an Excel file.

Zoom Controls – A slider and plus (+) and minus (−) buttons that let you zoom in or out of any Excel document so you view the contents more easily.

Troubleshooting guide